Cambridge Primary Path 6

Second Edition

Grammar and Writing Workbook

Garan Holcombe

Contents

Unit	Grammar	Learn to Write	Writing
1 What makes your region unique? page 3	Passive Voice Future Passive	Verbs Followed by Infinitives	Travel Brochure
2 Why do we seek adventure? page 13	Defining Relative Clauses Using *that* or *where* Defining Relative Clauses Using *who* or *whose*	Reflexive Pronouns	Diary Entry
3 How can we understand a work of art? page 23	Non-defining Relative Clauses *So, such; so … that, such … that*	Similes and Metaphors	Poem

Unit 1–3 Review page 93

Unit	Grammar	Learn to Write	Writing
4 How does information technology shape our lives? page 33	Reported Commands with *tell* and *ask* Reported Statements and Questions	*On the one hand, on the other hand*	Balanced Argument
5 How can we save the planet? page 43	Future Progressive *One, ones, some,* and *any* with Countable and Uncountable Nouns	*Because* and *since*	Explanation of How Something Works
6 What makes a good story? page 53	*Could have* and *should have* Past Perfect Simple	Colons and Semicolons	Micro-story

Unit 4–6 Review page 94

Unit	Grammar	Learn to Write	Writing
7 Why do we need medicine? page 63	Past Perfect Progressive Past Perfect Passive	*Before* and *after*	Informational Report
8 How do we use money? page 73	First and Second Conditionals Third Conditional	Quantifiers and Subject-Verb Agreement	Comparison Essay
9 How can we increase our brainpower? page 83	*If only* Modal Verbs of Deduction	Reporting Verbs	Memoir

Unit 7–9 Review page 95

1 What makes your region unique?

Grammar: Passive Voice

Geography Homework

Cally Bold, Class 2A
Monday, January 23

What makes your region unique? That's the question you asked us to answer for our geography homework, Mr. Walter. I told my parents about what we'd studied—the Arctic tundra, the world's great deserts, the Iban tribe of Borneo. But London's just a big, noisy city, I thought. What was unique about where I lived? I was given a history lesson!

The city of Londinium was founded by the Romans more than 2,000 years ago. In the 17th century, many of Shakespeare's plays were first performed here. In 1666, the city was almost completely destroyed by fire, but by the 19th century, it was the capital of an empire. Since then, it's only gotten bigger, and it is the center of British life.

Over many years, the city's culture has been transformed by immigrants from different countries. Hundreds of languages are spoken here. London is like a city, region, and country all in one—it's a world! That's what's special about where I live, Mr. Walters, and I think I'm seeing it for the first time!

1 Read Cally's homework assignment. When was London founded?

2 Complete the sentences. Each sentence uses a different form of the same verb. Which verb is it?

a I ____was given____ a history lesson.

b In the 17th century, many of Shakespeare's plays _____ first _____ here.

c In 1666, the city _____ almost completely _____ by fire.

d The city's culture _____ by immigrants from different countries.

e Hundreds of languages _____ here.

3

Grammar: Passive Voice

The passive voice is formed with the verb *to be* and the past participle of the verb (*developed*, *built*, *spoken*, and so on). We use it to focus on what happened rather than who or what was responsible for the action.

Compare these active and passive sentences in different tenses.

Present Simple Active
We serve breakfast between 7 and 9 a.m.

Present Simple Passive
Breakfast is served between 7 and 9 a.m.

Past Simple Active
Mom gave me a ukulele for my birthday.

Past Simple Passive
I was given a ukulele for my birthday.

Present Perfect Active
The storms have destroyed many buildings.

Present Perfect Passive
Many buildings have been destroyed by the storms.

Note that when we want to use the passive but also want to say who or what is responsible for the action, we use *by*.

3 Match the sentences with the tenses.

1 Present simple
2 Present simple passive
3 Past simple
4 Past simple passive
5 Present perfect
6 Present perfect passive

a Last summer, we went to China.
b The concert has been canceled.
c We've had a lot of tests this week.
d Every year we organize a fair in our neighborhood.
e The first iPhone was sold in 2007.
f An international arts festival is held in Edinburgh every August.

4 Complete the sentences with *is / are*, *was / were*, or *has been / have been*.

a The first Harry Potter book ____was____ published in 1997.
b In the last few weeks, several homes in our town _____ broken into.
c The Internet _____ developed in the second half of the twentieth century.
d A "ger" is an Inuit tent. It _____ taken down every time families move.
e My brother applied to a number of different colleges. So far he _____ accepted at two of them, but he is waiting to hear from the others.
f Every day, millions of videos and photographs _____ uploaded online.
g The houses on my street _____ built in the 1890s!

5) Complete the email with the verb in parentheses in the correct form.

Hi Uncle Sam,

Thanks for your email! You asked how everything is. Well, the region's changed so much since you were here. Ever since the Hollywood film that 1 ___was made___ (make) here three years ago, the town has been popular with tourists. Three new hotels 2 _____ (build) along the coast in the last eighteen months! Last summer, the roads to the main beach 3 _____ (block) for hours. We were on the news—Mom 4 _____ (interview) by a reporter! Mom misses the quiet days, but Dad says, "Places 5 _____ (improve) by tourists."

When are you coming to visit us? I know Australia is far away, but it would be great to see you!

Freddie

6) Complete the text with present simple passive, past simple passive, or present perfect passive forms of the verbs.

attend   make   light up   hold   ~~like~~

The Harbin International Snow and Ice Festival

Hello, blog readers! My last post 1 ___was liked___ 4,312 times! That's a new record, so thanks! Now, as you know, I love writing about my city of Harbin in the northeast of China. Today I'd like to tell you about the best thing here—the Harbin International Ice and Snow Festival! Every year, hundreds of thousands of people come to see our enormous ice sculptures of castles and monuments. In fact, last year, the festival 2 _____ by more than a million people! The festival 3 _____ in my city since 1983 and is celebrated every January. It lasts at least a month. Harbin is very cold—just right for sculptures made of ice! The sculptures 4 _____ by many people working together. Some of the biggest sculptures are produced by thousands of people. The best part of the festival is at night time, when the sculptures 5 _____. You must come to visit!

7) Use passive voice to write a short description of a festival in your country. Say when the festival was founded and when and where it is held. You might also describe what things are sold and what foods are eaten there.

_____
_____
_____

Grammar: Future Passive

DHC
Building the Future
DOW HUDSON CONSTRUCTION

Welcome to the Leisure Zone— The Future of Your Region!

We are pleased to announce a brand-new, multimillion-dollar development for the town of Greenville and the surrounding area. Work will begin this month. The complex will be opened to the public in May 2025.

The Leisure Zone is a unique, state-of-the-art complex, which will house restaurants, cafés, movie theaters, a shopping mall, a swimming pool, and the biggest gym in the state.

Key Facts

- The swimming pool will be 50 meters in length.
- The gym will be fitted with the latest equipment.
- Residents will be offered a specially reduced price to use the pool and gym.
- There will be more than 300 hundred shops in the mall.
- Movies will be shown in the complex's ten theaters from eight in the morning until midnight, every day of the week.

Anyone wishing to see a digital copy of the plans should go to leisurezone.com and click the link on the homepage. You will be taken to a 3-D plan of the complex, which will give you a good idea of what the Leisure Zone will look like.

1 Read the flyer. Has the Leisure Zone been opened yet?

2 Complete the sentences. Are they about the present or the future?

a The complex ___will be opened___ to the public in May 2025.

b The gym _____ with the latest equipment.

c Residents _____ a specially reduced price to use the pool and gym.

d Movies _____ in the complex's ten theaters from eight in the morning until midnight, every day of the week.

e You _____ to a 3-D plan of the complex, which will give you a good idea of what the Leisure Zone will look like.

Grammar: Future Passive

We can use the passive voice to talk about the future. We use the future simple of the verb *to be* and a past participle of the verb.

Breakfast will be served at the hotel between 7:00 and 9:30.

When will the new art museum be opened?

Remember: when we want to use the passive but also want to say who or what is responsible for the action, we use *by*.

I think in the future human beings will be controlled by robots.

3 Label each sentence *active* or *passive*.

a The school website will be updated next week. — passive
b My brother says he will go to live in Australia one day. — active
c Where will the next Olympic Games be held? — _____
d The movie theater will open in December. — _____
e Whoever wins the competition will be given a prize of $100! — _____
f My sister's book will be published in the summer. — _____
g When will you start at your new school? — _____

4 Complete the text with the future passive form of the verbs in parentheses.

School Drawing Competition!

We invite young artists to draw a picture on the theme of "my region." The art competition is open to everyone in the school.

Your drawings **1** will be judged (judge) by local artist Shay Lock. Five pictures **2** _____ (select) as winners, and there will be one overall winner. The five winning drawings **3** _____ (upload) onto the school website, and the five winners **4** _____ (give) a sketch pad and a set of beautiful drawing pencils.

The overall winning picture **5** _____ (put up) in the school hall in its own special frame.

Good luck, everyone!

5 Complete the text with the verbs in the future simple passive form.

Word box: ask, ~~show~~, give, decide, read

When I grow up, I'd like to be a writer and a filmmaker. This is what I imagine for my future ... My movies 1 __will be shown__ in theaters around the world. My stories 2 _____ by people in different countries. I 3 _____ by movie producers to turn my favorite books into movies. I 4 _____ a lot of awards for my books and movies. Of course, the truth is that my future 5 _____ by events beyond my control. But these are my dreams!

6 Rewrite the sentences in the future simple passive. Use *by* if a sentence indicates who or what is responsible for the action.

a They will open a new library in my town next month.
   A new library will be opened in my town next month.

b The British Museum will organize an exhibition on the Maasai of Kenya and Tanzania.
   _____

c Companies will develop many new technologies.
   _____

d They will build more houses near the park behind my school.
   _____

7 Use the information in the fact file and the future simple passive to make predictions about the future. Where there are no predictions in the fact file, make your own!

Topic	Prediction
quantum computers	solve problems quickly
changes in the climate	turn some places into deserts
astronomers	discover many new planets
robots	_____

a Problems will be solved quickly by quantum computers.

b _____

c _____

d _____

Improve Your Writing

Verbs Followed by Infinitives

Some verbs can be followed by infinitives (by *to do*, *to go*, *to see*, and so on). These verbs include verbs of thinking or feeling such as *want*, *forget*, *remember*, *like*, *love*, *hate*, *hope*, and *prefer*.

Don't forget to watch the video on the Berber of Africa, Class 3.
I hope to travel around the world when I'm older.

The negative is *not to* ...

I promised not to stay up late, so we decided not to watch the movie.

1 Complete the sentences with the correct form of the verbs in parentheses.

a _____Would_____ you _____like to watch_____ the documentary about the polar regions? **(would like / watch)**

b Yesterday, I _____ my schoolbag home. **(forget / bring)**

c My brother and his friends _____ around Asia this summer. **(want / travel)**

d Dad _____ when he was 35 years old. **(learn / drive)**

e Last night, I _____ my sister study for her math test. **(promise / help)**

2 Rewrite the sentences using the verbs. The new sentence must have the same meaning as the original one.

> remember ~~forget~~
> stay in   not be

a She never remembers to clean her soccer shoes.
She always _forgets to clean her soccer shoes._

b I promised to be on time for the party.
_____ late for the party.

c Since it was raining, we decided not to go out.
Since it was raining, we chose _____.

d I always forget to clean my room! I never _____!

3 Write three hopes you have for the future.

> _I hope to visit the Sahara desert one day!_

a _____

b _____

c _____

Writing: A Travel Brochure

1 READ Read the travel brochure. Where is Salar de Uyuni?

SALT AS FAR AS THE EYE CAN SEE

In the southwest of Bolivia, you'll find Salar de Uyuni. The largest salt flat* on the planet, it covers an area of 12,000 square kilometers and is 3,653 meters above sea level. In the middle of Salar de Uyuni there is a hill, on which cactus plants grow. The view from the top is amazing—it's as if you are surrounded by an enormous white sea. If you go on a special tour, you'll have a lot of time to explore.

- The nearest city to the salt flats is Uyuni. From there you can plan day or night tours.

- You can visit at any time. If you visit during the wet season, between December and March, when the hill gets flooded, you won't be able to climb it—but you will see the water lying on the salt and reflecting the sky like a mirror!

- If you go during the coldest months (June–September), remember to bring very warm clothes. It gets extremely cold. It's a good idea to take food and drink with you, too—you won't find any stores on the salt flats!

Why don't you plan your trip to Salar de Uyuni now? The people in the area will be happy to show you one of the world's great landscapes!

*A salt flat is an area of land covered with a layer of salt.

2 EXPLORE Complete the sentences.

> bullet points   catchy title   conclusion   facts

a A travel brochure needs a _____. This is what makes someone want to read it.

b Your description should include interesting _____, such as when something was built, how large the area is, or whether any historical figures have a connection to the place you're describing.

c You can use _____ to make practical information (e.g., when to visit and what to bring) much easier to read.

d Your _____ should try to make people want to visit the place you have described by offering them a welcoming invitation.

3 PLAN
You are going to write a travel brochure about a place in your country that you think people should visit. Complete the chart with some notes on the place.

Name of Place and the Region of Your Country It Is In

_____

_____

Description (what the place looks like, why it is worth visiting, interesting facts about it)

_____

_____

Practical Information (how to get there, best time of year to go, what to take)

_____

_____

4 WRITE
Write a travel brochure. Use your notes to help you.

_____

_____

_____

_____

CHECK
Did you …
- include a catchy title and welcoming conclusion ? ☐
- use bullet points with practical information? ☐
- describe the attraction and add interesting facts? ☐
- use verbs followed by infinitives if possible? ☐

Practice Your Exam Skills

Read this email from your friend Lucia and the notes you have made.

From: Lucia
Subject: My trip to Galicia in the north of Spain!

Hi Alvaro,

I can't wait to see you next week! I arrive at 3:00 p.m. on Monday.

Should I take the bus from the airport or take the train instead? — *Say we'll pick her up*

The landscape looks awesome in your photos! Can we walk in the mountains while I'm there? — *Yes if...*

I know everyone speaks Spanish in Galicia, but I'd like to know how to pronounce some words in Gallego so I can teach my friends back home here in Mexico City! — *Say I'll help*

Last thing: it rains a lot there, right? — *Yes! Bring a raincoat!*

See you soon,

Lucia

Write your email to Lucia using all the notes. Write about 100 words.

2 Why do we seek adventure?

Grammar: Defining Relative Clauses Using *that* or *where*

Blue Ridge Elementary School   June 12

Dear Parents,

We are pleased to announce a trip this summer to the Clear View Adventure Park. The trip is from Monday, August 11, to Friday, August 15, and costs $250. Previous trips to Clear View have been a great success.

Clear View is a place where young people can explore the natural world while learning important survival skills. Students will build a fire using dried grass. They will make a shelter that can protect them from the weather. They will also learn how to recognize plants that are safe to eat. It will be a lot of fun!

For more information, please contact me at the office or look online. ClearViewHub is the web page where Clear View keeps an archive of videos and reviews from visitors.

If your child would like to go, please register your interest by the end of the month. The form that you will need to complete can be found on the school website. Payment does not need to be made until the end of the semester.

Let the adventures begin!

Best wishes,

Maya Wright

---

1 Read the letter. How long is the trip to Clear View Adventure Park?

2 Complete the sentences. Then, look at the words you have added beginning with *that* or *where*. What word in the sentence do these added words give us more information about?

a Clear View is a place <u>where young people can explore the natural while learning important survival skills.</u>

b They will make a shelter _____

c They will also learn how to recognize plants _____

d ClearViewHub is the web page _____

e The form _____ can be found on the school website.

13

Grammar: Defining Relative Clauses Using *that* or *where*

A clause is a group of words including a subject and a verb. A relative clause begins with a relative pronoun such as *that*. It is used to give more information about a noun. When a relative clause adds essential information about a noun (information we need to understand what the noun refers to), it is called a defining relative clause. We use the relative pronoun *that* to add information about animals or objects.

   Bats are the only mammals that can fly.

   This is the book that will teach you the most about survival in the wild.

To add information about places, we use the relative pronoun *where*.

   Oh no, the theater where we saw the Batman movie closed.

3 Complete the sentences with *that* or *where*.

a   This is the town ____where____ my dad grew up.

b   Have you heard of the immortal jellyfish? It's the only animal _____ can make itself young again!

c   The musical instrument _____ my sister likes the best is our grandpa's 1962 Fender Telecaster guitar.

d   My friend moved to a school _____ he can focus more on science.

e   Look, this is a video about the museum _____ we saw the exhibition on Stone Age tools.

f   Mom works for a company _____ publishes children's books.

4 Complete the presentation with the phrases in the boxes.

> where we'll buy the food we need   that won't hurt your feet
> where we'll do some kayaking   that won't break after five minutes
> ~~where we'll build our shelters~~   where we'll do most of our exploring

OK, everyone, before we go on the trip, let's look at where we're going. If you look at the screen, you'll see a 3-D map. OK, this is the place where we'll camp. And this is the field 1 _where we'll build our shelters_. This is the lake 2 _____. And this is the forest 3 _____ _____. Through the trees there is the town 4 _____. Now, a word on equipment: Make sure you bring everything you need—a compass 5 _____, a sleeping bag that won't let water in if it rains, and a pair of boots 6 _____. Any questions?

14

5 **Write sentences using *that* or *where*.**

a compass / be / object / helps people figure out where they are

A compass is an object that helps people figure out where they are.

b bat / be / mammal / can fly

c kayak / be / type of canoe / was first used by the Inuit

d campsite / be / place / people set up their tents

e Rome / be / city / people can see many ancient ruins

6 **Change the two sentences into one using *that* or *where*.**

a The wild is a place. Animals like bears and lions live there.

The wild is the place where animals like bears and lions live.

b This is a river. We learned to fish here.

c Smoke signals are signs. They let others know where you are.

d This is a swimming pool. It has an amazing wave machine.

e This is a library. I met some famous writers here.

7 **Write sentences about objects or places that are important to you. Use *that* or *where*.**

Angharad's Park is the place where I learned to ride my bike.

The BMX was the bike that was the most fun to ride when I was young.

Grammar: Defining Relative Clauses Using *who* or *whose*

May and Ted

Mrs. Baker was the teacher who was teaching us that year. And there was one thing that Mrs. Baker loved: nature. One day, she said, "This morning, two people who have traveled the world are coming to visit us. They have an important message."

We'd never met any world travelers before. When May and Ted walked into the class, everyone went quiet. Ted said, "This is a woman whose home is the mountains." May said, "And this is a man whose life is the sea." We didn't really know what they were talking about, but we were fascinated.

"Once upon a time," said May, "the world was full of people who understood nature. They looked after it. And it looked after them. But today, we are excited only by technology. Ted and I would like to tell you to turn off your phones and tablets and look after the grass and the rivers, the fields and the trees, and the animals that we share our planet with."

From that moment on, my friends and I spent more and more time outside. We learned how to live in the wild—how to live with nature and take better care of it.

1 Read the story. What is the message that May and Ted share with the class?

2 Complete the sentences from the story. What do the words *who* and *whose* do in these sentences?

    a Mrs. Baker was the teacher _____ was teaching us that year.

    b This is a woman _____ home is the mountains.

    c This is a man _____ life is the sea.

    d The world was full of people _____ understood nature.

Grammar: Defining Relative Clauses Using *who* or *whose*

Defining relative clauses are used to add essential information about a noun. To add information about people, we use *who*.

There's the girl who won the school tennis competition last week!

To add information about possessions or things that in some way belong to someone or something, we use *whose*.

That's the house whose roof was blown off in the storm.

I spoke to the boy whose painting won the art competition.

3. Circle the correct word.

   a On the way home, we stopped to help a family **who / whose** car had broken down.

   b The driver **who / whose** knocked my brother off his bike called him to apologize.

   c Mr. Simmonds is the teacher **who / whose** YouTube videos have become really popular.

   d Apple and Microsoft are the companies **who / whose** products made home computing a reality.

   e The boy **who / whose** phone I found came to my house to get it. He was very happy!

   f Good news! Police have caught the men **who / whose** broke into the school.

4. Complete the email with *who* or *whose*.

Hi, Mom and Dad!

I'm writing this on the bus. Mr. Atkins told us about the sleeping plans. The boy 1 ___who___ I'm sharing a tent with is named Alex.

Next to me on the bus is the boy 2 _____ parents you were talking to at the mall the other day. His name's Karim.

Hey, you'll never guess what happened: Mr. Atkins sat on someone's bag by accident! The boy 3 _____ bag it was is named Jude. When Jude opened the bag, he saw his bananas had been squashed. Mr. Atkins was embarrassed. Mr. Atkins is the teacher 4 _____ phone fell in the lake on the last trip.

Paula is the girl 5 _____ is sitting next to Jude. She keeps complaining to Jude about the smell of squashed bananas.

OK, I've got to go! Here's a photo of me on the bus. The person 6 _____ took it is my friend Alice.

Love,

Ellis

5 Order the words to make sentences.

a the / there's / was / stolen / guitar / boy / whose
   There's the boy whose guitar was stolen.

b I / the / like / best / class / that's / whose / teacher
   _____

c who / girl / the / lives / a / on / riverboat / there's
   _____

d new / movie / boy / who / the / in / appeared / that's / Superman / the
   _____

6 Change the two sentences into one using *who* or *whose*.

a Walter is a boy. He won the school chess competition.
   Walter is the boy who won the school chess competition.

b Sam is a girl. She scored five goals in the last soccer match.
   _____

c Cameron is a boy. His aunt won an Oscar for costume design.
   _____

d Lacey is a girl. Her dad is a brain surgeon.
   _____

7 Write sentences about your friends. Use *who* and *whose*.

a the friend who speaks the best English
   Tom is the friend of mine who speaks the best English.

b the friend who most often asks you to do interesting things
   _____

c the friend whose house is nearest to yours
   _____

d the friend who gets the best grades on school exams
   _____

Improve Your Writing

Reflexive Pronouns

We use reflexive pronouns to show that the subject and object of the verb refer to the same person or thing.

My brother bought himself a new video game with his birthday money.
   subject   object

Leah and Danny taught themselves to play the piano.
      subject   object

Reflexive pronouns end in *-self* (if singular) or *-selves* (if plural):
myself   yourself   himself   herself   itself   ourselves   yourselves   themselves

1 Circle the correct reflexive pronoun.

a Our dog likes looking at **(itself)** / **ourselves** in the mirror!

b Leo fell off his bike yesterday and hurt **itself** / **himself**.

c In karate class, we learn how we can defend **itself** / **ourselves**.

d If you can't find a Spanish teacher, why don't you teach **yourself** / **itself**?

e See you later, you two. Enjoy **yourself** / **yourselves** at the party.

f Mom says she talks to **herself** / **ourselves** in order to have a good conversation!

2 Complete the dialogue with the correct reflexive pronouns.

Abbie I like this photo, Jack.

Jack I hurt 1 _____myself_____ building that fire.

Abbie What happened?

Jack I cut 2 _____ on some wood. But it was only a small cut.

Abbie Oh, you should be more careful. Please try not to hurt 3 _____, Jack… Did your dad like the camping trip?

Jack Yes, he did! He teaches 4 _____ new things whenever we go camping. This time, he learned how to find wild mushrooms.

Abbie Wow!

Jack He made 5 _____ some mushroom soup! It tasted awful.

Abbie Um … Jack … on the subject of food, could I have another one of those chocolate cookies, please?

Jack Of course! You can help 6 _____ to as many as you like, Abbie!

Writing: A Diary Entry

1 READ Read the letter. Who is Tom writing about?

Friday, August 15

It's the last day here at the Clear View Adventure Park. I've had an awesome week! I've been zip-lining, have built a fire, and have learned how to find edible plants. But the best part happened yesterday. Mr. Bridges took us on a river trip. The plan was to do some fishing.

Everything was going well until Anya and her friend Lara started arguing about who was going to take the next selfie with Anya's new camera. "You said I could take the next one!" shouted Lara. "But it's my camera!" shouted Anya. In the struggle, Lara slipped, stepped backwards, and knocked into Mr. Bridges, whose sun hat fell from his head and into the river. Oops!

Mr. Bridges stared at his hat as it bobbed around in the river. But Lara and Anya stopped fighting and went to work. Using a long, thin pole, they retrieved the hat from the water and returned it to a relieved Mr. Bridges! He reprimanded them for arguing but praised their quick thinking. Then, he posed for a photo wearing his soaking-wet hat! Anya put the photo on her Instagram page.

2 EXPLORE Match the excerpts from the diary entry to the key ideas about diary writing.

1 I've had an awesome week!
2 Lara slipped, stepped backwards, and knocked into Mr. Bridges
3 Friday, August 15

a main events described in the order they happened
b the date
c use of the first person and informal language

3 PLAN You are going to write a diary entry about something that you did or that happened recently—for example, a day out with family or friends, a trip to the movies, or something funny that happened at school. Make notes below.

Date

Main Events

Best/Worst/Funniest Thing About What Happened

4 WRITE Write your diary entry. Use your notes to help you.

CHECK

Did you …
- include a date? ☐
- use reflexive pronouns? ☐
- use an informal style in the first person? ☐
- describe the main events in the order they happened? ☐

Practice Your Exam Skills

Your English teacher has asked you to write a story.

Your story must begin with these sentences:
We were lost. It was getting dark, and the forest was a maze of trees.

Write your story. Write about 100 words.

3 How can we understand a work of art?

Grammar: Non-defining Relative Clauses

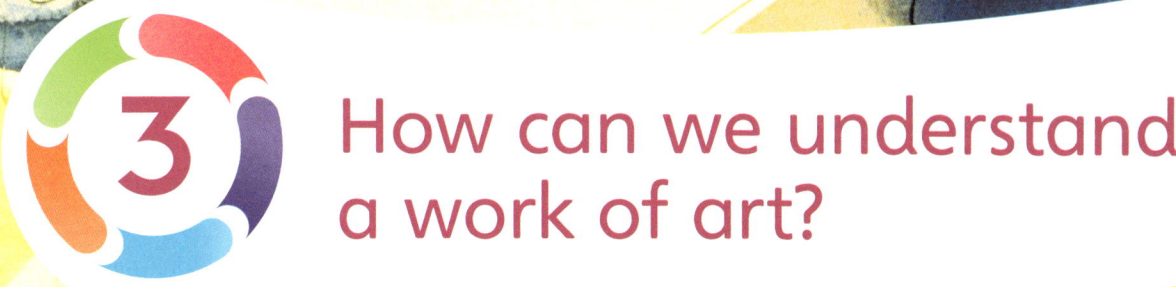

Art and My Family

Hello, I'm Daniela. Welcome to my blog, which is going to be all about art. Like everyone in my family, I *love* art. I like still lifes, landscapes, and portraits.

Speaking of my family, let me introduce them to you. We're all lovers of art! First of all, there's Mom, who likes paintings of people in rooms. For that reason, she likes paintings by Vilhelm Hammershoi and Johannes Vermeer. Then there's Dad, who prefers the abstract art of Mark Rothko and Wassily Kandinsky. He doesn't like realistic painting at all. "I don't understand why you think paintings of people in rooms are interesting," he says to Mom. Dad and Mom always disagree about art!

We live in Paris, where many famous artists have lived and painted—Picasso, van Gogh, Matisse. Our apartment is filled with prints of our favorite paintings. Mom, whose favorite painter is J. M. Turner, has a dream: she'd like to buy an original painting by one of the great masters like Rembrandt. But people spend millions of dollars on paintings by the world's most famous artists. We don't have that kind of money!

1 **Read Daniela's blog post. What is the dream of Daniela's mom?**

2 **Complete the sentences. What type of word completes each sentence?**

   a Welcome to my blog, _____which_____ is going to be all about art.

   b First of all, there's Mom, _____ likes paintings of people in rooms.

   c Then there's Dad, _____ prefers the abstract art of Mark Rothko and Wassily Kandinsky.

   d We live in Paris, _____ many famous artists have lived and painted.

   e Mom, _____ favorite painter is J. M. Turner, has a dream.

Grammar: Non-defining Relative Clauses

We use non-defining relative clauses to add information to a noun in a sentence. Commas around the clause indicate that the information in the clause is not essential.

In non-defining relative clauses, we use the relative pronouns *who*, *whose*, *which*, and *where*. *Who* is for people, *whose* is for possessions or for what in some way belongs to people, *which* is for things and places, and *where* is for places. (We do not use *that* with a non-defining relative clause.)

    Picasso, **who** was actually from Malaga, Spain, spent much of his life in Paris.

    Sam, **whose** father played soccer for Manchester United, has just been signed by Liverpool FC!

    Last week, we saw van Gogh's *The Starry Night*, **which** is in the Museum of Modern Art in New York.

    Krakow, **where** my cousin lives, is one of the most beautiful cities in Europe.

3 Circle the correct word.

  a We live next door to a man named Arnold White, **which / (who)** works at the museum in town.

  b That's Mrs. Reynolds, **whose / which** granddaughter is in my class.

  c My Aunt Robyn, **who / whose** studied art history at Princeton University, works as a professor.

  d Edinburgh, **which / where** my parents lived before I was born, is one of the most interesting cities in the U.K.

  e And this is the attic, **where / which** is my favorite room in the house.

4 Complete the text with *who*, *whose*, *which*, or *where*.

Mr. Brown, 1 _____who_____ I like very much, teaches us art, but whenever he tells us about the history of painting, 2 _____ is his favorite topic, he's always adding extra information to his sentences, 3 _____ makes his sentences very long. Mr. Brown, 4 _____ knowledge of the history of painting is excellent, often begins like this: "Today, class, we are going to talk about Salvador Dalí, 5 _____ was a surrealist, 6 _____ is what we call people who paint unusual things. Now Dalí, 7 _____ was from Catalonia, spent time in Paris, 8 _____ he met Picasso, 9 _____ was probably the most famous artist of the twentieth century, and in Paris, he ..." You get the idea! By the time we get to do some painting in the style of the artist Mr. Brown has talked about, everyone feels exhausted!

5) Complete the text with the phrases in the box.

> which I never play after seven o'clock in the evening   which is big enough to put the whole family in   ~~whose work takes her all over the world~~
> who works in a shed at the back of the yard   where I spend most of my time
> whose room I am going to have when he goes to college

OK, so you'd like to know what my family likes to complain about. Mom, **1** _whose work takes her all over the world_, likes complaining about airports. Dad, **2** _____, loves complaining about how cold his shed is. Actually, his shed, **3** _____, is warmer than the house! My brother, **4** _____, likes complaining about me! "You make too much noise," he says. I play the drums, you see. My drums, **5** _____, are quite loud. Me? I never complain! My room, **6** _____, is the happiest place in the house. I have my books, my video games, my paints, and my drums. What's there to complain about?!

6) Write sentences using *who*, *whose*, *which*, or *where*.

a My brother lives in Australia. Extra information: He is a journalist.

   My brother, who is a journalist, lives in Australia .

b We went to an awesome art exhibition. Extra information: It was at the Tate Modern.

   _____

c My friend Hannah is going to be in a movie. Extra information: She has been acting since she was five.

   _____

d This summer, we're going to Monterrey. Extra information: My uncle lives there.

   _____

e Our next-door neighbor is very kind. Extra information: Her cat always visits us.

   _____

7) Write about what people in your family do and like. Use non-defining relative clauses.

Mom, who is a doctor, likes reading. My sister, whose room is next to mine, is studying for her finals.

Grammar: *so, such; so ... that, such ... that*

The Life of Fenton Riley, Art Detective

Chapter One

Copying paintings and selling them is a crime. It's also such a big business that I am never out of work. Every year, criminals produce thousands of copies of famous paintings. These copies are often so good that they trick people into spending a lot of money. Later, those same people might worry that their painting is a fake. That's when they contact me—Fenton Riley, Art Detective.

It's my job to tell you if a painting is real or a forgery. This might sound easy, but it's not. In fact, it's so difficult that I can spend months studying a single painting. But don't get me wrong—I'm very lucky to have such an interesting job. When I was asked if I'd like to write a book about it, I said yes right away. I was so happy!

In these pages, I will tell you how to be a good Art Detective. To begin, we need to learn about the history of art. Let us begin, then, by going on a journey back in time ...

1 Read the opening page of Fenton Riley's book. What does he say you need to do to be a good art detective?

2 Read the text again. Complete the sentences from the text with *so (that)* or *such (that)*. Which word goes before an adjective and which goes before an adjective + noun?

a It's also ____such____ a big business ____that____ I am never out of work.

b These copies are often _____ good _____ they trick people into spending a lot of money.

c In fact, it's _____ difficult _____ I can spend months studying a single painting.

d I'm very lucky to have _____ an interesting job.

e I was _____ happy!

Grammar: *so, such; so ... that, such ... that*

So and *such* are similar to *very* because we use them to intensify the quality of an adjective or adverb.

    I'm **so** sleepy.

    This is **such** an awesome book!

We use *so* before an adjective (e.g., *tired*, *hot*) or adverb (e.g., *fast*, *quietly*, *beautifully*). We use *such* before an adjective + noun (*a famous artist*, *delicious food*).

We can use sentences with *so ... that* and *such ... that* to describe a cause and effect.

    It was **so** cold **that** we decided to stay at home.

    (cause: very cold weather; effect: deciding to stay at home)

3 Circle the correct word.

a This is **so** / **such** a beautiful painting. It's called *Portrait of a Man*, and it's by Rembrandt.

b My Uncle Marco speaks **so** / **such** loudly.

c Oh, no, we're **so** / **such** late! Come on, let's go.

d We had **so** / **such** a good time at Amelia's party.

e Mmmmm, this is **so** / **such** delicious ice cream!

4 Transform the sentences using *so* or *such*.

a It was such a good trip to Florence.

The trip was _____ *so good* _____.

b We stayed at such an awesome hotel.

Our hotel was _____.

c The food was so tasty.

We ate _____.

d The art we saw was so beautiful

We saw _____.

e We met such nice people.

The people we met were _____.

5 Use *so ... that* or *such ... that* and the words in parentheses to complete the sentences.

a It's ___so hot that___ I'm finding it hard to sleep. (**hot**)
b The TV show was _____ I fell asleep. (**boring**)
c Eve is _____ a _____ runner _____ she wins every race. (**fast**)
d We had _____ a _____ time in Türkiye _____ we're going back. (**good**)
e Conrad speaks _____ I can hardly hear him. (**quietly**)

6 Make one sentence from two. Use *so ... that* or *such ... that*.

a I was tired. I stayed at home.
   I was so tired that I stayed at home.
b It was hot. We went swimming in the ocean.
   _____
c The book was amazing. I read it again.
   _____
d It was beautiful weather. We went out all the time.
   _____
e It was a terrible movie. We left before it ended.
   _____

7 You went to an art exhibition. Everything went wrong! Use the information, your own ideas, and *so*, *such*, *so ... that*, and *such ... that* to write about the trip.

Part of the Trip	Description
the ticket	expensive
the line	long, took an hour to get to the museum
the tour guide	spoke quietly, couldn't hear what she said
the exhibition room	dark, couldn't see the paintings very well
the food in the museum café	
the train home	

The ticket to the exhibition was so expensive.

Improve Your Writing

Similes and Metaphors

We use similes and metaphors to describe one thing in terms of something else. In a simile, we use the words *like* or *as* to make a direct comparison between the two things. In a metaphor, we say that one thing is something else. Poets and novelists often use similes and metaphors to help us see things in a new way.

Metaphor:
That man **is a dragon**.

Simile:
That man **is like a dragon**.
That man is **as angry as a dragon**.

1 Identify the sentences as metaphors or similes.

a   The snow was a blanket upon the bed of the winter fields.   metaphor
b   Your face is like a screen full of emoticons.   _____
c   Our house was a zoo, and my brothers were the monkeys.   _____
d   The clouds were travelers in an empty sea.   _____
e   The children sang like birds on the first morning of spring.   _____
f   You're like an app that won't download.   _____

2 Match the phrases to complete the common similes.

1   as fast   a   as honey
2   as sweet   b   as an elephant
3   as green   c   as the sky
4   as blue   d   as ice
5   as cold   e   as grass
6   as big   f   as lightning

3 Write your own similes. Complete each simile with a single noun (e.g., *a dog*) or a phrase (e.g., *a dog in the park on a sunny day*).

a   It was as hot as _____.
b   I was tired as _____.
c   My friends were as happy as _____.

Writing: A Poem

1 READ Read the poem. What does Mr. Jewel think of Jocasta-May Greene's painting?

The man on the TV, talking to me,
Is angry, so angry, a wild summer bee.
"This isn't art!" says the man to the screen,
And he points to the artist, Jocasta-May Greene.
"She doesn't know how to paint or to draw.
She's a child without skill. Yes, I've told you before.
I could do this myself, oh, anyone could.
I could do this myself, and I probably should."

But Jocasta-May Greene is calm as a cat.
She smiles, and she touches the rim of her hat.
"Mr. Jewel," she says, "my art's not for you.
It is abstract in style, and for you that won't do.
But I'm happy to watch you paint something yourself.
My paints and my brushes are there on that shelf,
So please come and show me just where I've gone wrong;
I'd so love to know how awesome art sings its song."

2 EXPLORE Complete the text with the words in the box.

lines   rhyme   capital letter   ~~verses~~   syllables

How Poems Are Organized

Poems are usually organized into groups of lines called 1 ___verses___. There may be four or more 2 _____ in each verse. Poems often have a special rhythm, which is how the poem sounds when it is read. Poets often achieve this rhythm by thinking about how many 3 _____ there are in each word and in each line as a whole. Many poems 4 _____ (use words that end with the same sound, e.g., *cat* and *ha*t), but not all poems do. Often, each new line in a poem begins with a 5 _____, but again, this is the choice of the individual poet.

3 PLAN You are going to add a verse to the following poem. Before you do that, complete the first verse with the phrases in the box.

> I'm a camera   from Neptune to Mars
> The sky's like a book   the night that I see

The Astronomer

_____ that I read through its stars,

All the stories of planets _____,

I'm a camera recording _____,

_____ but not taking photos of me.

4 Complete the chart to plan your verse.

Write some words to describe the nighttime sky.	
Use a metaphor or simile to describe the sky.	
Use a metaphor or simile to describe the stars.	
Write some words to describe what the person in the photograph thinks of the nighttime sky.	

5 WRITE Write a second verse of the poem. Include a simile and a metaphor.

_____
_____
_____
_____
_____
_____

CHECK

Did you ...
- write a complete verse? ☐
- use rhyming words? ☐
- use a simile and a metaphor? ☐
- begin each new line with a capital letter? ☐

Practice Your Exam Skills

Complete the text. Write one word in each blank.

My Life as an Artist

I started painting when I 1 ___was___ three years old. Since then I haven't stopped. I was lucky to grow up in Madrid, 2 _____ there are several awesome museums.

The painting that has inspired me the most is *Las Meninas* by Velázquez, 3 _____ is my favorite artist. You can see the painting in Madrid's El Prado museum.

When I was eighteen, I moved 4 _____ Scotland, where I attended the Glasgow School of Art. I graduated three years ago and now live in Berlin. It's 5 _____ an exciting city. I sell my paintings online and organize exhibitions of my work in cafés. I do still lifes, and I also do portraits 6 _____ people I know, especially my friends and family.

4 How does information technology shape our lives?

Grammar: Reported Commands with *tell* and *ask*

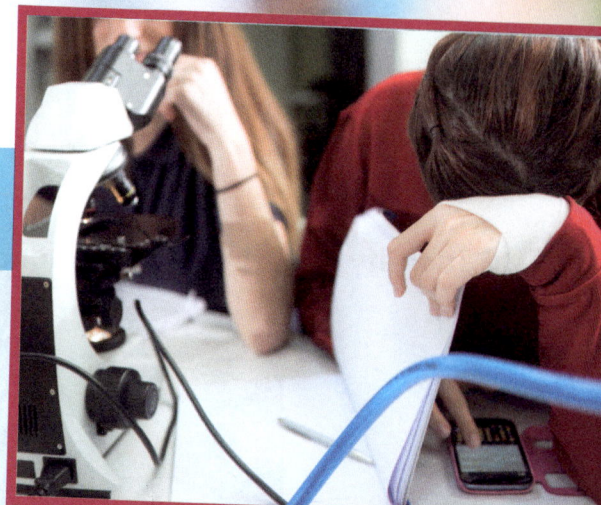

Kasia's Diary

Wednesday, December 5

This morning, in IT class, Mr. Dawes asked us to talk about smartphones. He put us in small groups, and he asked each group to choose a chairperson, whose job it would be to start the discussion and keep it going. Then, he told the chairpeople to have someone take notes on their group's ideas.

In our group, the chairperson was Ruby. "Well," she said, "I think the worst thing about smartphones is that people never turn them off." Mr. Dawes told Ruby not to talk so loudly. She said, "Sorry, Mr. Dawes," and then asked the group if we agreed with her. I was about to say that I disagreed when I heard a computerized voice say, "You have a new message." It seemed to be coming from under a notebook on the desk. "Oh!" said Ruby. "That's … " "Does someone have a phone in class?" asked Mr. Dawes. Everyone looked at Ruby. Mr. Dawes asked her to put her smartphone on his desk. "Can I just check my message?" said Ruby. Mr. Dawes didn't answer, but we could see from the expression on his face what the answer to that question was.

1 Read Kasia's diary entry. Who uses their smartphone in class?

2 Complete the sentences. In each sentence, what type of verb is used after *tell* and *ask*?

   a Mr. Dawes asked us _____ about smartphones.
   b He asked each group _____ a chairperson.
   c He told the chairpeople _____ someone take notes on their group's ideas.
   d Mr. Dawes told Ruby _____ so loudly.
   e Mr. Dawes asked her _____ her smartphone on his desk.

Grammar: Reported Commands with *tell* and *ask*

In addition to using *tell* to introduce reported statements and *ask* to introduce reported questions, we use *tell* and *ask* to introduce reported commands. For reported commands, we need the infinitive after *tell* or *ask* and need an object (e.g., *us*, *students*) between *tell* or *ask* and the infinitive.

Direct Command	Reported Command
"Study hard for the IT exam."	Our teacher **told** us **to study** hard for the IT exam.
"Don't use your phone in class."	The teacher **asked** students **not to use** their phone in class.

3 Identify the reported commands, reported statements, and reported questions.

a The teacher told me to click on the icon.   reported command

b Mom asked me where her bag was.   _____

c Dad told me to stop it.   _____

d Mr. Jackson told me he liked reading books about computers.   _____

e Dad asked me what grade I got on my IT exam.   _____

f The teacher asked us to be quiet.   _____

4 Complete the sentences. In each sentence, what type of verb is used after *tell* and *ask*?

> not talk   do   not use   ~~not take~~   clean   not play

a My sister told me ___not to take___ her tablet to school without asking her.

b Mom told me _____ my smartphone at night.

c Dad asked me _____ my room.

d Dad told me _____ my homework before watching TV.

e Mom asked me _____ so loudly at the dinner table.

f My brother asked me _____ games on his computer.

5) Report the commands. Use the words in parentheses.

a "Please hand in your projects on Monday." **(teacher / tell / class)**
The teacher told the class to hand in their projects on Monday.

b "Please close the door." **(teacher / ask / Sean)**

c "Hurry up!" **(Mom / tell / Dad)**

d "Get some rest." **(doctor / tell / my sister)**

e "Please don't be late!" **(Jack / ask / us)**

6) Read the underlined sentences. Report four things Henry's parents told him to do.

I wish my parents would stop saying "do this" or "don't do that." I know it's their job, but after a long day in school, it can be tiring to come home and get even more commands. Take yesterday, for example. As soon as I got home, Mom said, "Take off your shoes, Henry." Then, Dad said, "Do your homework." Then, Mom said, "Set the table for dinner." Then, Dad said, "Wash the dishes." Then, Mom said, "Dry the dishes." My mom and dad are very nice people, but I think they should use the word *please* once in a while. *Hmmm.* Now how can I ask them to do that?

a
b
c
d

7) Report four things your parents have recently told you or asked you to do.

Grammar: Reported Statements and Questions

Brandon's Blog About Video Games

It happened last Monday. In the morning, in IT, Mr. Winterson mentioned that he played video games, and he said that his favorite game was Avenger. Then, he mentioned that he was on Level 5. I couldn't believe it! I asked him how to get to Level 5. He explained that you had to go incredibly fast into the Black Tunnel of Cranmore—so fast that the Great Green Blob wouldn't know where you were or what you were doing. I asked him what happened on Level 5. He just smiled and said, "Wait and see."

When I got home from school, I went up to my room. I logged in to Avenger and went through Levels 1, 2, and 3. In Level 4, I went more quickly into the Black Tunnel of Cranmore than ever before and … instead of looking out from my room and into the game, I was looking out from the game and into my room! I was inside Avenger! I know it's hard to believe, but it's true!

If you'd like to know what happened next, leave a comment. If I get to 1,000 comments, I'll continue the story of my incredible adventure …

1 Read Brandon's blog post. How many comments would Brandon like to get on his post?

2 Complete the sentences. Which of these verbs are used to report a statement, and which ones are used to report a question?

   a Mr. Winterson ____mentioned____ that he played video games.

   b He _____ that he was on Level 5.

   c I _____ him how to get to Level 5.

   d He _____ that you had to go incredibly fast into the Black Tunnel of Cranmore.

   e I _____ him what happened on Level 5.

Grammar: Reported Statements and Questions

When reporting statements, we often use *said* and *told*, but we can also use verbs like *mention* and *explain*. When reporting questions, we usually use *asked*.
Remember! As these examples show, in reported statements and questions we usually put present tense verbs into past tenses and change pronouns and possessive adjectives.

"I have a blog."   Brandon mentioned that he had a blog.
"My blog's about video games."   He explained that his blog was about video games.
"What is the URL?"   I asked Brandon what the URL was.

Remember! When we report questions, we usually change the order of the words. When we report *yes/no* questions, we usually use *if* after *asked*.

"What is your blog called?"
Ryan asked.   Ryan asked Brandon what his blog was called.

"Do you use emojis?"
asked Grace.   Grace asked Brandon if he used emojis.

3 Circle the correct verb.

a I **asked / (mentioned)** that I wanted to work for a technology company when I was older, like the people in the photo.

b The teacher **explained / asked** that the World Wide Web was created in 1989 and helped make the Internet popular.

c Dad **asked / mentioned** that he had two tickets to the Lakers game. I couldn't believe it!

d James **explained / asked** me if I wanted to go to the movies after school.

e I **asked / mentioned** my friend how many social media accounts she had. She said she didn't know!

4 Report the statements. Use the verb in parentheses. Make all the necessary changes.

a "I have my own blog." **(mentioned)**
I _____ mentioned that I had my own blog _____.

b "I don't like social media." **(explained)**
Mom _____.

c "My daughter works for Apple in Cupertino, California." **(mentioned)**
Mr. Smith _____.

d "I don't have a smartphone." **(mentioned)**
Jacob _____.

e "I'm building a website for my family's bookstore." **(explained)**
Sarah _____.

5 Report the questions. Make all the necessary changes to the sentences.

a "When was the Internet invented?"
   I asked Miss Warner _____ when the Internet was invented _____.

b "Do you use Instagram?"
   My friend asked me _____.

c "Where is my tablet?"
   My brother asked me _____.

d "Do you have a Facebook account?"
   The teacher asked us _____.

e "What do you think of virtual reality games?"
   My sister asked me _____.

6 Report the underlined parts of the conversation.

a **Zach** Do you like Ben's video?

b **Jasmine** Yes, I do! I think it's very funny.

c **Zach** Ben doesn't want to keep on making videos about movies.
   Jasmine Why not?

d **Zach** He wants to do something different. This is his last video about a movie.

a Zach asked Jasmine if she liked Ben's video.

b Jasmine said _____

c Zach mentioned _____

d Zach explained _____

7 Think of or imagine a conversation you have had about what you like and dislike about technology and report it. Try to use *say*, *tell*, *ask*, *mention*, and *explain*.

Jacob and I talked about YouTube. I mentioned that I watched YouTube videos every day. Jacob explained that he didn't like YouTube because he thinks that most of the videos on it aren't interesting or funny.

_____
_____
_____
_____

Improve Your Writing

On the one hand, on the other hand

We use the expressions *on the one hand* and *on the other hand* when we are contrasting two different facts or different ways of thinking about something.

On the one hand, smartphones are awesome. **On the other hand**, we spend too much time using them.

1 Complete the sentences with the phrases.

> it isn't good for the environment
> ~~it makes them much more complicated~~
> it can be hard work to take care of one
> it makes it difficult for stores in towns to survive
> we have too many exams

a On the one hand, technology makes our lives easier. On the other hand, _it makes them much more complicated_.

b On the one hand, I'd love to have a pet, like a cat or a dog. On the other hand, _____.

c On the one hand, the Internet makes buying things easier. On the other hand, _____.

d On the one hand, flying means we can travel long distances quickly. On the other hand, _____.

e On the one hand, I really enjoy school. On the other hand, _____.

2 Rewrite three of the four sentences with *on the one hand ... on the other hand*. Find the sentence that can't be rewritten using the phrases.

a Social media is fun, but it can waste your time.
On the one hand, social media is fun. On the other hand, it can waste your time.

b Video games are awesome; however, many of them are too violent.

c There is so much information online, but we don't know if it's true.

d I enjoy playing soccer, and I'm good at it.

e Although it's easy to meet people online, the Internet can make us feel lonely.

Writing: A Balanced Argument

1 READ Read the essay. Choose the best title.
- a Do We Understand Social Media?
- b Should We Stop Using Social Media?
- c Can Social Media Change the World?

1 Every day, billions of messages are sent around the world; it has never been easier to contact others. However, some people are worried that applications like Facebook and Instagram make us sad rather than happy. Should we should stop using them? Let's consider the arguments.

2 On the one hand, social media is the perfect communication tool. It's enjoyable to use, and it lets us stay in touch with old friends and make new ones. Online, it is easy to find a community of people who share our interests. This is the argument that social media brings people closer together.

3 On the other hand, paying too much attention to posts on social media can be a problem. It can seem as if the people we follow online have perfect lives, better than the one we are living. Social media, says this argument, can't be a replacement for face-to-face connection with other human beings.

4 Although social media is entertaining, we should learn to understand the difference between the "virtual" friendships we make through it and the "real" ones we have offline. There is no need to stop using social media, but we would all benefit from understanding what it is—a useful way of contacting people, but not something we should spend all our time using.

2 EXPLORE Match each paragraph of the essay to a description of its content.

1 Paragraph 1   a arguments against social media
2 Paragraph 2   b conclusion and short summary
3 Paragraph 3   c arguments for social media
4 Paragraph 4   d introduction to the topic

3 **PLAN** You are going to write an essay. Choose one of the following topics to write about, and then make notes on it.

Should children under ten be allowed to use smartphones and tablets?
Should we encourage people to read books instead of e-books?
Should we use computers more in schools?

a Introduction to the topic

b Arguments for

c Arguments against

d Conclusion and short summary

4 **WRITE** Write your essay. Use your notes to help you.

CHECK

Did you ...
- introduce the topic? ☐
- include arguments for the idea? ☐
- include arguments against the idea? ☐
- write a conclusion and a short summary? ☐
- use *on the one hand ... on the other hand*? ☐

Practice Your Exam Skills

Five sentences have been removed from the text below. Complete the text with the missing sentences. There are three sentences that you do not need to use.

Is It Smart to Have a Phone?

My parents didn't really want me to have a smartphone. I had to convince them it was a good idea. **1** _____ Then, I mentioned that I was the only 13-year-old I knew who didn't have one. In the end, they bought me a smartphone for my fourteenth birthday, but they told me to be careful about how I used it.

I'm 15 now, and I'm not so sure that I want to have a smartphone. Like with anything, there are benefits and there are drawbacks. **2** _____ On the other hand, I spend too much time looking at a screen. **3** _____

I know that smartphones are useful. **4** _____ I want to break free from it! I spend hour after hour on social media, posting photos and talking to my friends. **5** _____ Although it's good to know what my friends are thinking, I sometimes think I should just put my phone down and do something else. But it's so hard to stop looking at the screen. Do you have the same problem?

a Chatting online is so addictive.
b Spending hours in front of a screen can make you feel very tired.
c I first explained that all of my friends had one.
d I most enjoy looking at videos.
e On the one hand, I have all the entertainment I need.
f But I feel tied to mine, almost as if I am its prisoner.
g My sister has had the same phone for years.
h After that, I dropped my phone and its screen broke.

5 How can we save the planet?

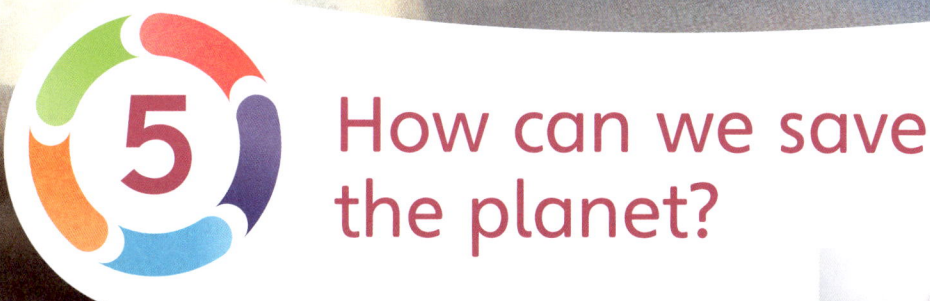

Grammar: Future Progressive

▶ BE THE CHANGE YOU WANT TO SEE

Our environment reporter spoke to Bonnie Lewis, whose *Wake Up!*, a book about global warming, has been a bestseller around the world.

Why did you write this book?

I used to think human beings would find clever solutions to the problem of burning fossil fuels. I'd say, "In a hundred years' time, people will be living on a healthy planet." But the more I learned about the problem, the more I realized that we can't leave the solution to others. If we do, there will be more pollution, more days of extreme heat, more terrible storms and floods.

What does the future hold for the planet?

If we continue on in the same way, by 2050, millions of people will be searching for new places to live. It's that serious.

What can people do?

Our economies are based on making, buying, and selling more and more things. This has to change. We must live more sustainable lives. If we don't change, one thing is clear: by the end of the century people won't be living, they'll be surviving. But we can change, and that's what my book is really all about.

On December 3, Bonnie Lewis will be speaking at the United Nations Conference on Climate Change in New York. Tickets are available online.

1 Read the interview. What does Bonnie say her book is really all about?

2 Read the interview again. Match the time phrase to the action.

1 In a hundred years' time
2 By 2050
3 By the end of the century
4 On December 3

a people won't be living, they'll be surviving
b Bonnie will be speaking in New York
c millions of people will be searching for new places to live
d people will be living on a healthy planet, Bonnie had thought

Grammar: Future Progressive

We use the future progressive to describe actions that will be taking place at a time in the future. The future progressive is formed with *will be* and the present participle of the verb. Time expressions such as *next year*, *soon*, *this time next week*, and *by the summer* are frequently used with the future progressive.

Will human beings **be living** on another planet by the end of the century?

This time next week, my grandparents **will be traveling** to Los Angeles.

I **won't be playing** in the tennis tournament this weekend. I've injured my knee.

When using the future progressive, we often use contractions of *will* (e.g., *I'll*, *won't*).

3 Complete the conversations with the verbs in the box in the future progressive.

> catch   wait   ~~take~~   stand   arrive

Charlie I can't believe I'm going to the climate change conference!

Mom Let's talk through the plan again. We **1** _will be taking_ you to the station in the morning. You **2** _____ the train at 7:30, and you **3** _____ at Grand Central Station at 9:30.

Charlie 4 _____ Uncle Jack _____ for me at the station?

Mom Yes, that's right. He **5** _____ by the big clock there. And he'll walk with you.

4 Write questions in the future progressive form. Write full answers in response.

a   where / Charlie / go / tomorrow morning

Where will Charlie be going tomorrow morning?
Charlie will be going to the climate change conference.

b   who / drive / Charlie / to the station

_____?
_____

c   what time / Charlie / get the train

_____?
_____

d   what time / Charlie / get in to Grand Central

_____?
_____

5 Use the words in parentheses to complete the dialogues with sentences in the future progressive.

1. **A** Would you like to come over to my house tomorrow after school?
   B I can't. _____ in the tennis tournament. **(I / play)**

2. **A** _____ to Luke's birthday party on Friday?
   B Yes, I think so. It starts at five o'clock, doesn't it? **(you / go)**

3. **A** This time next week _____ in Switzerland.
   B I know! I can't wait! **(we / ski)**

4. **A** Did I tell you? _____ to college in the fall.
   B Why not? **(my sister / not go)**

6 Read. Then, use the future progressive to write four ideas about what we will and won't be doing in 2060.

Life in 2060

How we will be living in 2060? Will we all be using solar power? Will we be driving cars, or will we be getting around on foot or by bike? Will we still be taking long flights from one part of the world to another? Will we even be living on planet Earth? Perhaps the only thing we know is that we won't be living as we live now—things will be different. Tell me your ideas about what we will and won't be doing. You can choose from the following six topics.

Transportation   Food   Home   Music   Technology   The Planet

_____
_____
_____
_____

7 Answer the questions about your life. Use the future progressive.

a. What will you be doing this Saturday afternoon? _____
_____

b. Where will you be going on vacation next summer? _____
_____

Grammar: *one*, *ones*, *some*, and *any* with Countable and Uncountable Nouns

NATURE MAGAZINE
ESSAY-WRITING COMPETITION

My Thoughts on Planet Earth by Jamie Winterson

Global warming *is* real. The problems we are experiencing—the ones we hear about every day, such as more extreme weather and the melting of the polar ice caps—are not going to disappear. We need to remember that our planet is the only one we can live on.

We live as if we have all the time in the world; soon, we won't have any. If we go on burning fossil fuels, cutting down our forests, and polluting our rivers, there will come a time when life on Earth becomes more difficult and dangerous for every living thing on it.

We know what the problems are, but what about the solutions? Well, Bonnie Lewis has some. I've just finished her book *Wake Up!* I don't usually feel different after reading a book, but I did after reading this one. Bonnie is right. We all have to do something before it's too late. So, I'm going to stop eating meat and dairy products, reduce the waste I produce, and walk and bicycle more. I can do more, but it's a start. We all need to start somewhere.

25

1. Read the essay. What did Jamie feel after he had read *Wake Up!*?

2. Read the sentences from the essay. The highlighted words replace another word from earlier in the sentence or paragraph. Which words do they replace?

   a. The problems we are experiencing—the **ones** we hear about every day, of more extreme weather and the melting of the polar ice caps—are not going to disappear. _____problems_____

   b. We need to remember that our planet is the only **one** we can live on. _____

   c. We live as if we have all the time in the world; soon, we won't have **any**. _____

   d. We know what the problems are, but what are the solutions? Well, Bonnie Lewis has **some**. _____

   e. I don't usually feel different after reading a book, but I did after reading this **one**. _____

46

Grammar: *one*, *ones*, *some*, and *any* with Countable and Uncountable Nouns

One, *ones*, *some*, and *any* are used to avoid repeating a noun. We use singular *one* and plural *ones* for countable nouns (e.g., *river*, *tree*, *table*).

My tablet broke, so I bought a new one. (instead of *so I bought a new tablet*)
I'm looking for hiking boots like the ones you have on display in the window.

We use *ones* only with other information (e.g., *the ones in the window*, *new ones*). If there is no other information, we use *some/any* rather than *ones*.

I need big envelopes. Could I have some, please? NOT Could I have ones, please?

We use *any* and *some* for countable nouns and uncountable nouns (e.g., *water*, *money*, *time*). In general, we use *any* in negative sentences and *some* in positive sentences.

We don't have any eggs, and we need some for breakfast.
If we want to travel around the world, we need money, and we don't have any!

3 Circle the correct word in the dialogues.

1. **A** Is this a good video game?
   B Well, it's OK, but if I were you, I'd get this **(one)** / **ones**.

2. **A** Dad, what do you think of that bass guitar?
   B It's OK, but take a look at this old **one** / **ones**!

3. **A** Could I have two muffins, please?
   B Yes, of course. Which **one** / **ones** would you like?

4. **A** I don't like these gloves.
   B What about the black **one** / **ones**?

5. **A** Can I help?
   B Yes, please. Can you put this vase on the table and that **one** / **ones** on the windowsill?

4 Complete the sentences with *some* or *any*.

a. Are you looking for cookies? I think there are _____some_____ in the cupboard.
b. I think we need more paintings for the living room. Let's look for _____.
c. Oh, no! We need juice for the party. I just realized we don't have _____.
d. That milkshake looks good. Can I try _____?
e. If you need stamps, look in the desk. I'm sure there are _____ in there.
f. I bought two new T-shirts, but Isabel didn't buy _____.

5 Complete the email with *some*, *any*, *one*, and *ones*.

Dear students,

I am writing to tell you how proud I am of you for having spoken at last week's UN Conference on Climate Change. As you said, our way of life has become destructive; we need a new 1 ____one____ ! The problems we face, the 2 _____ you described in such detail, are very big— 3 _____ seem impossible to solve. As you told the conference, we need solutions, and too often our politicians don't offer 4 _____. But if we follow the suggestions you made, we can start to make a small difference.

Your inspiring speeches made me believe that another world is possible, 5 _____ in which we each do our best to help preserve the planet for future generations. After all, this planet is the only 6 _____ we have!

Yours,

Miranda Ballard, Principal, Washington Elementary

send

6 Rewrite the sentences by replacing the repeated noun.

a Look after the planet. It is the only planet we have.
   Look after the planet. It is the only one we have.

b I like a lot of authors, but the author I like the most is George Orwell.
   _____.

c I have so many books—I can lend you books.
   _____.

d We need milk—could you buy milk?
   _____.

e These glass bottles are better to use than those plastic bottles.
   _____.

f I would lend you money, but I don't have money.
   _____.

7 Answer the questions with your ideas.

a Planet Earth has many problems. Which ones do you think are the most serious?
   The ones I think are the most serious are global warming and the destruction of rain forests.
   _____

b Of all the ideas you have heard about how to solve the problem of climate change, which one do you think is the best?
   _____

Improve Your Writing

Because and since

We use the conjunctions *because* and *since* to give reasons for something and to connect causes with effects. In general, when we wish to focus more on the effect than the cause, we use *since*, and when we wish to focus more on the cause than the effect, we use *because*.

Since I'm not feeling very well, I'm not going to the birthday party.
We didn't go to the park **because** it was raining.

1 **Make one sentence using *because*.**

a We wanted to learn about planet Earth. We went to the exhibition.
We _____ went to the exhibition because we wanted to learn about planet Earth _____.

b Jon lost the tennis match. He is disappointed.
Jon _____.

c Milly is studying very hard. She has a big math exam tomorrow.
Milly _____.

d We wanted to see the *Mona Lisa*. We visited the Louvre.
We _____.

e Our train was delayed. We got home late.
We _____.

f I go swimming five days a week. Exercise is very important.
I _____.

2 **Make one sentence using *since*.**

a I'm going to the movies. I've finished my homework.
Since I've finished my homework, I'm going to the movies.

b My parents bought me a new video game. I did very well on my exams.
_____.

c I'm learning Mandarin. We're going to live in Beijing.
_____.

d I was feeling very hungry. I had two slices of cake.
_____.

e We went to the beach. The weather was awesome.
_____.

f I am tired. I am going to bed.
_____.

Writing: An Explanation of How Something Works

1 READ Read about the invention. What does it do?

The Garbage Tube

Since there is garbage everywhere—in our fields, on our streets, and outside our stores—we need something to get rid of it. That is why we have invented a product called the Garbage Tube. It is perfect for large open spaces like parks because it lets you clean up quickly and it isn't too heavy. How does it work? Read and find out.

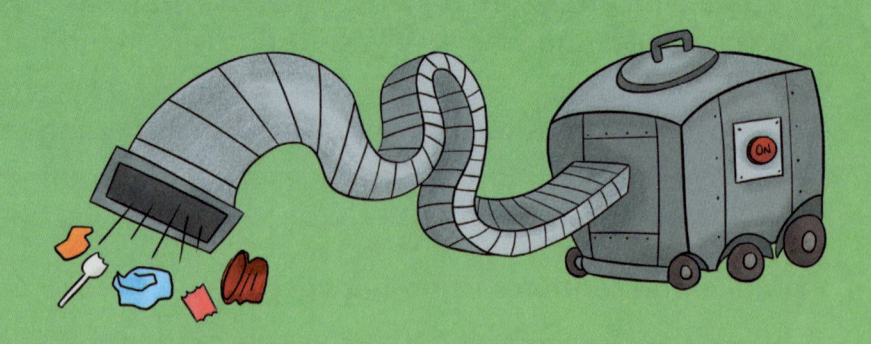

1 The design of the Garbage Tube is based on the vacuum cleaners we all have in our homes. It consists of a long, wide tube that is attached to a metal container. You hold the tube in one hand and the container in the other.

2 There is a button on the side of the Garbage Tube. To switch the tube on, you press this button and then hover over an item of garbage. The item is sucked up into the metal container.

3 When the metal container is full, an alarm sounds. At this point, the container can be detached from the tube and opened, after which the garbage can be deposited in a trash can.

4 Once the metal container is empty, you re-attach it to the tube. Then, you can keep on cleaning up your town!

2 EXPLORE Complete the sentences.

> present tense   numbered steps   connectors   diagrams   introduction

a An _____ to a product or process gives the reader a basic understanding of the product or process that the rest of the text will describe at greater length.

b An explanation of a product or process often includes _____, which make the information easier for the reader to follow.

c Explanations are usually written in the _____.

d _____ are words like *when*, *then*, *since*, and *because*. We use them to make information in an explanation easier to read.

e _____ are very useful, as they give people the opportunity to see what the text describes.

3 PLAN You are going to write an explanation of how something works. Invent an object that could be used to help the environment in some way (for example, a recycling machine, a machine to make seawater drinkable, a machine to remove plastic from the oceans). Complete the graphic organizer with notes.

Name of Object
_____

Introduction
_____
_____

Numbered Steps

1 _____
2 _____
3 _____
4 _____

4 WRITE Use the graphic organizer to write your explanation of how the object works in your notebook. Draw and label a diagram of the object.

CHECK

Did you ...
- write an introduction? ☐
- use the present tense? ☐
- draw a diagram? ☐
- include numbered steps? ☐
- use connectors? ☐

Practice Your Exam Skills

ARTICLES WANTED!
Save Planet Earth

What problems does the planet face? What do you do to help the environment? Do you do enough?

Write an article answering these questions. The author of the winning article receives a copy of *Life on Earth* by David Attenborough!

Write your article. Write about 100 words.

6 What makes a good story?

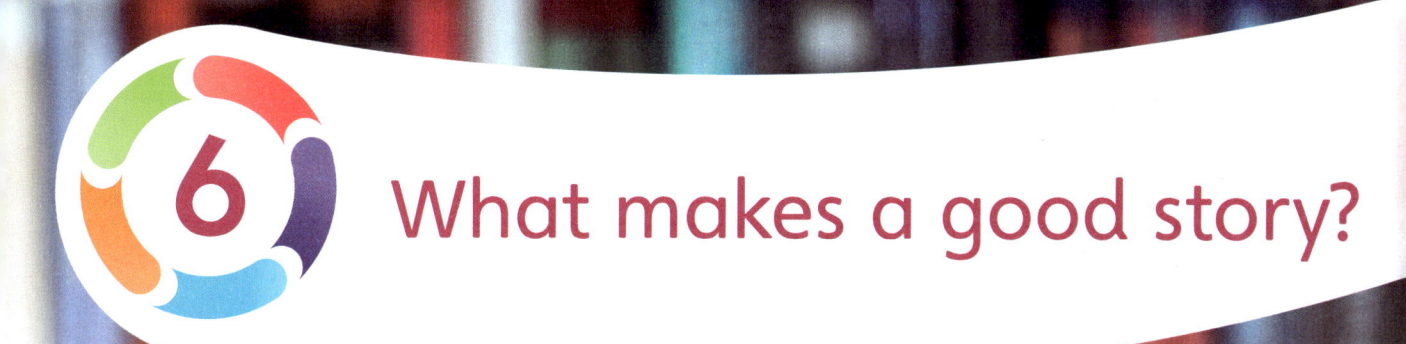

Grammar: *could have* and *should have*

The Man Who Didn't Listen

For Mr. Brown, who taught us English literature, nothing his students did was good enough. He always had an idea, some suggestion or advice about the past—about something we could have done, or should have done, or shouldn't have done. When I got a bad grade on an exam (the questions were about Charles Dickens, and I didn't know as much about Charles Dickens as I did about J. K. Rowling), Mr. Brown said, "You should have studied more, Samantha" and "You could have read my book about Charles Dickens."

Mr. Brown wanted the students to listen to him, but he didn't really want to listen to them. One day, at the start of class, the students were all talking loudly about the author Philip Pullman and his amazing *His Dark Materials* trilogy and wondering if Mr. Brown liked the books, too. "Stop talking!" he said. "You shouldn't have joined my literature class. None of you is interested in literature!" "But we're talking about literature, Mr. Brown," said Freddie. "Oh," he said. "Are you? Well, you could have told me!"

1 Read the story. What were the students in the class talking about?

2 Read the story again. Complete the sentences. Are the sentences about the past, present, or future?

　a　You _____ studied more, Samantha.
　b　You _____ read my book about Charles Dickens.
　c　You _____ joined my literature class!
　d　Well, you _____ told me!

Grammar: *could have* and *should have*

Could have and *should have* are followed by the past participle (*written*, *watched*, etc.). We use *could have* to make deductions about the past. We are not sure what happened, but we believe that the action we mention was a possibility.

I don't know where my key is. It could have fallen out of my jacket pocket.

We also use *could have* for suggestions about the past—about actions that were possible but did not happen.

I could have bought the black sneakers, but I decided to buy the red ones instead.

This use often expresses regret or criticism about what happened or didn't happen.

Oh, no! We could have seen the movie after all. It was playing at the mall.
I didn't know it was a swimming pool party, Jacob. You could have told me!

Should have is stronger than *could have*. We often use *should have* and *shouldn't have* to express regret or give advice about what happened or didn't happen.

A: I didn't do well on my exam, Dad. I should have done better.
B: Yeah, you should have studied more. You shouldn't have waited until the end.

3 Complete the sentences with *could have* and a verb from the box.

> play   leave   buy   go   ~~say~~   hurt

a Misha! You ___could have said___ you have the new J. K. Rowling book! Can I look at it?
b Look in your room for your book, Meg. You _____ it on your bed.
c Tom's OK, but he _____ himself. He fell all the way down the stairs.
d I didn't know you liked tennis, Nicola. You _____ with us.
e You _____ the black jeans, you know. They looked great on you!
f My brother _____ to Yale University, but he decided not to.

4 Complete the sentences with *should have* or *shouldn't have*.

a I ___shouldn't have___ shouted at my little brother. It's always better to stay calm.
b It's going to rain. I _____ brought an umbrella.
c Oh no! All the tickets have been sold. We _____ waited so long to buy them.
d I feel too full. I _____ eaten so many slices of chocolate cake.
e Joe _____ come with us. He would have loved this movie.

5) Complete the dialogue with the phrases in the box.

> shouldn't have looked should have called could have helped
> could have been ~~shouldn't have stayed up~~

Ben Oh, I'm so tired, Lucy. I went to bed at 11:00.

Lucy Really? You 1 _shouldn't have stayed up_ late, Ben.

Ben I was studying for the exam. But I didn't really understand what I was reading.

Lucy You 2 _____ me! I 3 _____ you.

Ben That 4 _____ fun.

Lucy English is my best subject, remember!

Ben The worst thing was that I looked on the Internet.

Lucy You 5 _____ at the screen that late, Ben.

Ben More good advice! Maybe I'll listen to you one day, Lucy.

6) Rewrite the sentences using the words in parentheses.

a I wish we had gone to the beach last weekend. (could have)
   We could have gone to the beach last weekend.

b It would have been a good idea for us to go by train. (should have)
   _____.

c It was a bad idea for you to eat so many sweets. (shouldn't have)
   _____.

d Maybe you left your book at school. (could have)
   _____.

e I had enough money to buy the black jacket. (could have)
   _____.

7) Think about a recent mistake you made. Think about what you could have done, should have done, and shouldn't have done. Write four sentences.

I shouldn't have bought that computer. I could have looked at different computers.

Grammar: Past Perfect Simple

A Biography of Philip Pullman

Philip Pullman, who was born in Norwich, England, in 1946, is one of the United Kingdom's most popular authors. Although literature had been his passion since his childhood, when he graduated from college, he became a teacher. By the time his first children's book came out, in 1982, he had been teaching for several years.

He continued to publish stories, and by the mid-1990s, he had published more than fifteen books. However, these books hadn't prepared him for what came next in his career. With the publication of the *His Dark Materials* trilogy—fantasy novels that tell the story of Lyra and Will as they travel in different universes—Philip Pullman became a famous author.

The *Amber Spyglass*, the final book in the trilogy, was published in 2000. Like the first two books, *Northern Lights* and *The Subtle Knife*, which had come out in 1995 and 1997, it was an enormous success. In fact, in 2001, *The Amber Spyglass* won the Whitbread Award. This was an incredible achievement for the author, as it was the first time that the award had gone to a children's novel.

1 Read the biography of Philip Pullman. Which of Philip Pullman's books won the Whitbread Award?

2 Read the biography again. Complete the sentences.

  a Although literature _____had been_____ his passion since his childhood, when he graduated from college, he became a teacher.

  b He continued to publish stories, and by the mid-1990s, he _____ more than fifteen books.

  c However, these books _____ him for what came next in his career.

  d Like the first two books, which _____ in 1995 and 1997, it was an enormous success.

  e This was an incredible achievement for the author, as it was the first time that the award _____ to a children's novel.

56

Grammar: Past Perfect Simple

We use the past perfect simple to describe an action that takes place before another action or time in the past. The past perfect simple is formed with *had / hadn't* and the past participle of the verb.

   Maria Gonzalez had won three big tennis tournaments by the time she was 16 years old.

   When we got to the swimming pool, it had already closed.

   Finn struggled on the exam because he hadn't studied enough for it.

Notice that the action that comes later in time is expressed with the past simple (*was*, *got*, and *struggled* in the examples).

3 Complete the dialogues with the words in parentheses. Use the past perfect form.

a A Did your brother enjoy the Tolkien book?
   B Yes, he did. ___He hadn't read___ any of his books before.   (he / not / read)

b A Did you see Lisa at the party?
   B No, I didn't. _____ by the time I got there.   (she / go)

c A Did you manage to catch your train?
   B No, I didn't. _____ by the time I got there.   (it / leave)

d A Did you enjoy your trip to London?
   B Yes, we did. _____ there before.   (we / not / be)

e A Did the exam go well?
   B No, it didn't. _____ enough for it.   (I / not / study)

4 Complete the sentences with the verbs in parentheses. Decide which action comes first and put one verb in the past perfect form and one verb in the past simple form.

a When we ___got___ (get) to the movie theater, we discovered that it ___had closed down___ (close down).

b It _____ (be) great to see my cousins last summer because I _____ (not see) them for a long time.

c Karl _____ (not want) anything to eat because he _____ just _____ lunch (have).

d By the time he _____ (be) 25, Alessandro Bianchi _____ (write) four novels for children.

e We _____ (get) to the theater so late that the show _____ already _____ (start).

5 Complete the sentences with the information. Use a past perfect verb and a past simple verb.

a My friends left the park. Then, I arrived at the park.
By the time <u>I arrived at the park, my friends had left</u>.

b I worked in Mexico for a few months. Then, I started learning Spanish.
After _____.

c Dad made breakfast. Lucy got up after that.
By the time _____.

d Sam ate lunch. Soon after that, Jon got to the café.
When Jon _____.

e The bus left the station. We arrived at the station.
When we _____.

6 Complete the sentences with the information. Use a past perfect verb and a past simple verb.

The Noise in the Night

need   pull   see   ~~be~~   hear

It was late. I **1** <u>had been</u> awake for a long time. Now I really **2** _____ to get some sleep, but how could I go to sleep when there was a strange noise coming from the garden? I **3** _____ this noise earlier in the night—a noise like a bear. It couldn't be a bear, could it? Although we lived in the Rocky Mountains in Canada, I **4** _____ never _____ a bear before tonight. I told myself to be brave, and I **5** _____ back the curtains. There was my brother in the middle of the lawn! "What are you doing?" I said. "Practicing!" said my brother. "Didn't you know? I'm playing a brown bear in the school play. It's called *The Bear in the Nighttime!*"

7 Write a short description of something you did last weekend. Use the past simple and the past perfect.

<u>Last weekend I played soccer in the park. When I got to the park, my friends had already arrived.</u>

Improve Your Writing

Colons and Semicolons

We use the colon (:) to introduce a list, an example, or a piece of information that expands on what goes before it.

    This is what we need for the party: bread, cheese, cake, and balloons.

    My grandfather's advice for life is simple: do what you love doing.

We use the semicolon (;) to separate two parts of a sentence that are related and could each be written as a separate sentence.

    I opened the door and walked in; the room was cold.

    (I opened the door and walked in. The room was cold.)

1 Add a colon to each of the sentences.

a There is only one place in the world I would really love to visit: Egypt!

b The United Kingdom is made up of four countries England, Scotland, Northern Ireland, and Wales.

c To make this chocolate cake, you will only need a few ingredients eggs, flour, butter, baking powder, sugar, and some delicious dark chocolate.

d We came back from town with so many things three new books, some pencils, a notepad, a jigsaw puzzle for my sister, and a new pair of slippers for my dad.

e There are two things you need to know about this town it's very cold in the winter and very hot in the summer.

f To win this match today, we only need one thing self-belief!

2 Add a semicolon to each of the sentences.

a We have final exams soon I have to study all weekend.

   We have final exams soon; I have to study all weekend.

b The rain kept falling we were getting wet.

c My sister is going to live in Canada she got a job there.

d Europe is a fascinating continent it has so many different cultures.

e I'm not going to Marco's party after school I don't feel very well.

f I enjoyed the story I think I'll read more of her books.

Writing: A Micro-story

1 READ Read the micro-story. Who was the surprise person at Suzie's birthday party?

The Dress

She'd never know. I'd wear my sister's dress to the party, and my sister would never know.

Suzie was having a dress-up birthday party, but I had nothing beautiful to wear; I only had old jeans and T-shirts. That's when I got my idea: I could wear my sister's black dress! Although my sister was five years older than me, we were the same height; her dress would fit me perfectly.

Walking to Suzie's house, I felt great. And I kept feeling great until my sister opened Suzie's front door. "What are you doing here?!" I said. "Suzie's parents hired me to be a waitress at the party. But I've got a question for you, Carrie: What are you doing in my dress?"

2 EXPLORE Complete the text with the words in the box.

> resolution   action   ~~micro-story~~   exciting   beginning

What is a micro-story?

A 1 __micro-story__ is a very short story, often no longer than a hundred words. The 2 _____ of this type of story needs to be 3 _____ or interesting in some way. There should be a problem or a secret of some kind—something to hold the reader's attention. The 4 _____ should then build until we get to the 5 _____, which ends the story by solving the problem or revealing the secret.

3 PLAN   You are going to write a micro-story. Before you write it, think of your ideas and make some notes.

Title	
Main Characters	
Setting	
Problem or Secret That Begins the Story	
Main Action	
Resolution	

4 WRITE   Write your micro-story. Write about 100 words.

___

CHECK

Did you …
- write a beginning to capture the interest of the reader? ☐
- write a resolution and build the action before the resolution? ☐
- use colons or semicolons, if possible? ☐

Practice Your Exam Skills

The people below all want to read a new book. Read the descriptions of books that have just been published. Decide which book would be the most suitable for the people below.

1. Jen's favorite genre is the mystery story. She likes having a problem to solve and seeing if she can work it out by the end of the book. Jen likes poems, but she doesn't enjoy stories set in space.

2. Erica especially enjoys reading stories about space. Although she likes poetry and fairy tales, her favorite genre is science fiction. She would rather read about the future than the past.

3. Mo likes history and often reads stories about the kings and queens of the past, but he prefers poetry to other kinds of literature. He enjoys the rhythm of poetry, and he especially likes poems that rhyme.

4. Alex likes mysteries and science fiction, but they aren't his first choice of things to read. Since he was a young child, he has really enjoyed reading fairy tales; he likes the fact that they involve magic.

New Books

A *Long Live Prince Cal*
It is 301 BCE. When King Ruthlebert the Second dies, his kingdom is attacked by the Lords of the Far Seas. Only young Prince Cal, the old king's only son, can save the people of the Five Kingdoms. But Prince Cal doesn't want to be king.

B *The Old House at the End of Cherry Lane*
No one knows what is wrong with the old house at the end of Cherry Lane. But everyone knows that there is something wrong. Who lives inside, what do they want, and why are the streetlights in the town of Mudbridge going off one by one?

C *The Door at the End of Time*
Jay Blake, astronaut, physicist, and host of popular TV programs about the universe, wakes up one morning to find himself in a large pod on the surface of the moon. How did he get there, and how can he get back home?

D *Grimm in the 21st Century*
This collection takes the famous stories of the Brothers Grimm "Cinderella," "Sleeping Beauty," "Snow White"—and updates them. Now, princesses rescue princes, dragons are sometimes frightened, and stepmothers are friendly and kind.

E *Songs for Tomorrow*
A new collection by Helen Boswell, whose simple but powerful poems about nature have become popular around the world. These poems offer the reader something new: they are the first in which the poet has used rhyme.

7 Why do we need medicine?

Grammar: Past Perfect Progressive

I probably should have stayed at home last Monday. I hadn't been feeling well for days, but I thought it was just a bad cold.

In school, we had been learning about medicine and why we need it. Mr. Shears had told us about famous people like Hippocrates and Florence Nightingale. I'd been enjoying learning about medicine and wanted to know more. But when Mr. Shears asked, "Are you OK, Abby?" I realized that other people in class also had been asking me that question. "Um," I said, "actually, I don't think so."

I ended up in the hospital, where I was diagnosed with the influenza virus. "You have a very bad strain of it," said the doctor. I was trying hard to hold on to her words. She'd been talking to me for a while before I understood what she was saying. "The virus makes you feel very, very tired," she explained. "It can be difficult to concentrate." A few days later, when I was feeling a little better, I asked the doctor why she had decided to study medicine. "Oh, that's an easy one," she said. "I wanted to help people feel better!"

1 Read Abby's story. How had she been feeling before the Monday she went to the hospital?

2 Read the story again. Complete the sentences. Are the verbs for actions that happened in a moment or over a period of time?

a I _____ well for days, but I thought it was just a bad cold.

b In school, we _____ about medicine.

c I _____ learning about medicine …

d She _____ to me for a while before I understood …

Grammar: Past Perfect Progressive

We use the past perfect progressive to describe an event or action in the past that was still continuing at the time of another event, which is often expressed in the past simple. We use *had been* and the present participle of the verb. *Had been* is often used in its contracted form, *'d been*.

> We **had been playing** soccer in the park when it started to rain.
> I **hadn't been feeling** very well, so I went to the doctor.
> I was feeling tired. I **had been working** hard all day.

3 Make sentences in the past perfect progressive.

a We / learn / Spanish / for three years
   <u>We had been learning Spanish for three years</u>.

b We / wait / for the train for two hours
   _____.

c Grandpa / sleep / since lunchtime
   _____.

d We / swim / all afternoon
   _____.

e I / watch TV / for a long time
   _____.

4 Complete the sentences with the words in the box. Use the past perfect progressive form.

> not play   stand   live   study   wait   ~~work~~

a By the time Mom decided to change careers and become a doctor, she <u>had been working</u> as a journalist for fifteen years.

b James was in a bad mood. He already _____ an hour for his bus to come.

c My clothes were soaked. I _____ in the rain for an hour. I wanted to watch the soccer match, but I wish I'd brought my umbrella!

d My sister _____ in New York for years before she visited the Metropolitan Museum of Art.

e My cousin Pablo _____ soccer professionally for very long before he was asked to play for the Spanish national team.

f I was feeling tired. I _____ for my exam all morning.

5 Put the verbs in parentheses into the past perfect progressive or the past simple form.

a My sister _had been following_ tennis for a long time, so she was delighted when she _____got_____ tickets to the Wimbledon final. (follow) (get)

b We _____ basketball on the new court but _____ because it was too hot. (play) (stop)

c We _____ the mountain for an hour when it _____ to snow. (climb) (start)

d By the time we got to Melbourne, we _____ exhausted. We _____ for almost 24 hours! (be) (travel)

e Alba was out of breath when she _____ at school. She _____ for half an hour. (arrive) (run)

6 Complete the text with the words in the box. Use the past simple or past perfect progressive form.

> sleep ~~be~~ find
> know work

Sleeping on the Job

It was Friday evening. I **1** _____was_____ so tired. By then, I **2** _____ for 17 hours without a break! Both Mom and Dad were doctors, so I **3** _____ life in the medical profession was difficult. But, as a new doctor, I wasn't prepared for the reality of it.

I needed a rest, so I **4** _____ an empty room and lay down on the sofa. But by the time Suzanne woke me, I **5** _____ for two hours! Although Suzanne didn't say anything to him, the head doctor found out and scolded me. It was a long, long time before I had another rest at work!

7 Write about the last time you went to the doctor. How had you been feeling before the appointment? Include some verbs in the past perfect progressive in your description.

I last went to see the doctor in January. I hadn't been feeling very well for a few days. I had been coughing and sneezing. The doctor told me I had a bad cold, and she gave me some medicine.

_____

_____

Grammar: Past Perfect Passive

Tales of the 21st Century
The Hospital at the End of Town

We had been told that things would get better. But President John was wrong. After the problems, people started to leave our country in search of a better life.

By the time my family decided to leave, everything had become worse. The streets hadn't been cleaned for months. The garbage hadn't been collected for weeks. Schools had been closed down one by one. And boards had been put on the windows of the schools. The doctors in the hospital had tried to continue their work, but they hadn't been given the resources they needed. In the end, the United Nations had arranged for patients to be treated in other countries. It's all very sad, really, but I'm not writing this to be sad. I have a plan, you see.

One day, when I grow up and am a young woman, I am going to study medicine and become a doctor. I will then return to my hometown and re-open the hospital that I was born in. I don't care how long it takes to make things better. I'll keep going. That's what good doctors do.

1 Read the story. What does the girl want to do when she grows up?

2 Read the story again. Complete the sentences. How are these verbs different in form from past perfect active verbs?

  a We ___had been told___ that things would get better.
  b The streets _____ for months.
  c The garbage _____ for weeks.
  d Schools _____ one by one.
  e The doctors in the hospital had tried to continue their work, but they _____ the resources they needed.

Grammar: Past Perfect Passive

We use the passive voice when we want to focus on what happened rather than on who or what was responsible for the action, often because this who or what is either unknown or unimportant.

When we got back to the hotel, we were surprised to discover that the room hadn't been cleaned.

We form the past perfect passive with *had been* and the past participle of the verb (*said*, *written*, *invented*, and so on).

Compare the passive and active forms of the past perfect:

Past Perfect Passive	We had been told that the hospital was going to close.
Past Perfect Active	Someone had told us that the hospital was going to close.

3 Circle the correct choice: past perfect passive or past perfect active.

a Everyone loved the birthday cake. It **(had been made)** / **had made** with Grandpa's recipe.

b The bus **had been canceled** / **had canceled**. How would we get home?

c I was surprised. Mr. Thomas **hadn't been told** / **hadn't told** us that we had a biology exam.

d My sister **had been finished** / **had finished** her project on the human body. She was tired.

e We told the police that our bags **had been stolen** / **had stolen**.

f By the time I logged on to the website, the theater **had been sold** / **had sold** all the tickets.

4 Complete the sentences with the verbs in the box and *had been* or *hadn't been*.

> invite   broke   send   ~~open~~   cancel

a The new hospital _had been opened_ officially by the mayor. Mom applied for a job as a nurse there.

b Despite what it said on the website, we were told that the show _____. We were happy!

c Although we _____, we didn't go the party.

d The teachers were angry because a window in the gym _____.

e The bookstore told me that my books _____ yet. They said they'll mail them right away.

5 Write sentences in the past perfect passive.

a The hotel room / reserve
   The hotel room had been reserved.

b The flight tickets / buy
   _____.

c The bags / pack
   _____.

d The house / lock up
   _____.

e The dog / take / to Grandma's
   _____.
   They were ready to go!

6 Transform the sentences from the past perfect active to the past perfect passive.

a They had opened a new hospital.
   A new hospital had been opened.

b They had painted the walls yellow.
   _____.

c They had cleaned the rooms.
   _____.

d They had hired more nurses.
   _____.

e They had bought more equipment.
   _____.

7 While your parents were out, you and your brother spent the afternoon cleaning the house. Use the past perfect passive to write about which chores had and hadn't been done by the time your parents got home. Include a chore of your own that had been done and one that hadn't.

do the dishes ✓
straighten up the bedrooms ✓
clean the kitchen ✗
take out the garbage ✓
do the laundry ✗
vacuum the rugs ✓
_____ ✓
_____ ✓

By the time our parents came home, the dishes had been done.
The bedrooms _____

Improve Your Writing

Before and after

We use *before* and *after* to order events in the past, the present, or the future.

Before you answer the exam questions, please read the questions very carefully.
You need to finish your science homework **before** dinner, Alistair.
I went to my friend's house **after** school.
After watching the movie, we went to get pizza.

1 Complete the biography with *before* or *after*.

The Life of Jonas Salk

Jonas Salk was born in New York in 1914. **1** _____ he began work at the University of Michigan in 1942, he studied medicine at New York University, from which he got his medical degree in 1939. **2** _____ working at the University of Michigan for a few years, he became an associate professor of bacteriology at the University of Pittsburgh, which he joined in 1947. It was at Pittsburgh that Salk began studying polio, a disease of the nervous system, which was affecting many young people in the middle of the 20th century. **3** _____ he could develop a successful vaccine for polio, he and other scientists had to work hard in order to understand the disease. Finally, in 1955, Salk's vaccine was introduced in the U.S.A. **4** _____ its introduction, the number of people getting polio fell. **5** _____ this success in combating polio, Jonas Salk moved to San Diego's Institute of Biological Studies, which was later renamed the Salk Institute.

2 Write one sentence using the word in parentheses.

a   We had lunch. Then, we went for a walk. (after)
    After we had lunch, we went for a walk.

b   I was born on the 19th. My friend was born on the 22nd. (before)
    _____.

c   Antibiotics were discovered. The disease could be cured. (after)
    _____.

d   I washed my hands. Then, I ate the sandwich. (after)
    _____.

e   It wasn't 9:00 yet. I went to bed. (before)
    _____.

Writing: An Informational Report

1 READ Read the report. Can everyone have an MRI scan?

Report Topic: MRI Scan

What Is MRI? MRI stands for Magnetic Resonance Imaging. An MRI scan uses magnetic fields and radio waves to produce an image of the body. This type of scan allows doctors to look inside a human body without using an X-ray. Almost any part of the body can be scanned using MRI.

When Were MRI Scans First Performed? The first MRI scan was performed by Dr. Raymond Damadian in 1977. With two of his students, Dr. Damadian built the first machine that was big enough for a human body.

What Happens During a Scan? During an MRI scan, the patient lies on a bed, which is then moved into the scanning machine. The machine is controlled by a technician who the patient can talk to. A scan lasts anywhere from fifteen minutes to an hour and a half, and the patient must keep still throughout the process. The scanner makes loud noises, but patients are able to wear earplugs or headphones.

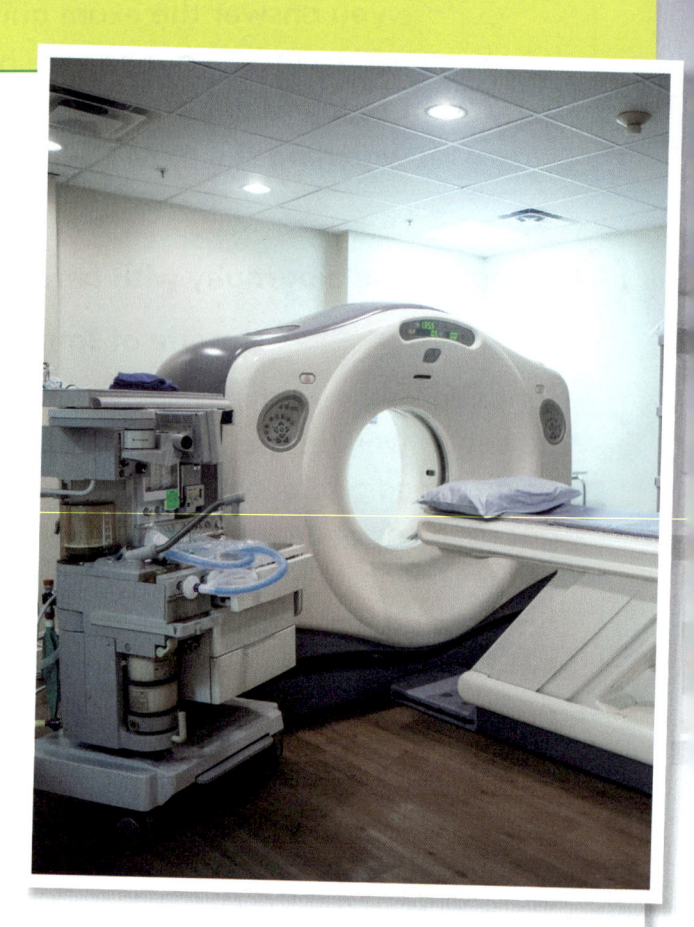

Are MRI Scanners Safe? Although some people may find it uncomfortable to be inside the machine, MRI scans are safe. However, people who have metal implants should not have this type of scan.

2 EXPLORE Complete the text with the words in the box.

> subtitles   introduction   third person   paragraphs   formal   images

HOW TO WRITE AN INFORMATIONAL REPORT

An informational report should begin with a short 1 _____ to the topic. The main information in the report should then be organized into 2 _____ under 3 _____. One or more 4 _____ should be used to illustrate the report in order to make it easier for the reader to understand what is being described. Finally, remember that an informational report is a 5 _____ text and should be written in the 6 _____.

3 PLAN
You are going to write an informational report about an object that doctors use. Research one of the objects below. Complete the table with the information.

A stethoscope   **B** thermometer   **C** reflex hammer

What Is It? What Is It Used For?	
When Was It Invented and Who Invented It?	
How Is It Used?	
How Does It Help a Doctor? Why Is It Important?	

4 WRITE
Use the information in Activity 3 to write your informational report.

CHECK
Did you …
- write an introduction?
- use the third person?
- organize information into subtitled paragraphs?
- use *before* and *after*, if relevant?

Practice Your Exam Skills

Choose the correct answer: A, B, or C.

HAVE YOU WASHED YOUR HANDS?

Help us provide the best care and avoid the spread of superbugs. Please use the new antibacterial gel found throughout the hospital.

Dad! The hospital changed the time of my appointment. It's at 3:00 now, instead of 2:00. Can you pick me up later than planned—at, say, 4:00? Cassie x

---

1 The hospital is informing visitors

A that there is a superbug in the hospital.

B of a way to prevent the spread of superbugs.

C that they must provide their own antibacterial gel.

2 Cassie is contacting her father to

A tell him what time she'll pick him up.

B remind him about the original time of the appointment.

C suggest a different time for him to come get her.

APPLICATIONS TO DANVERS MEDICAL SCHOOL MUST BE SUBMITTED BY THE END OF SEPTEMBER. APPLICATIONS CAN BE MADE ON THE WEBSITE OR BY COMPLETING A PAPER FORM AND HANDING IT IN TO THE OFFICE.

Hi Evie,

I'll be back late this evening. (I'm going to a welcome party for the trainee nurses.) Please help Dad get the twins to bed. See you later.

Love, Mom

---

3 A Students should only apply online.

B Students must complete a paper form.

C Students can choose how they want to apply.

4 A Evie's mom would like Evie to help at home.

B Evie's dad would like some help with the party.

C Evie's mom would like the twins to help her.

8 How do we use money?

Grammar: First and Second Conditional

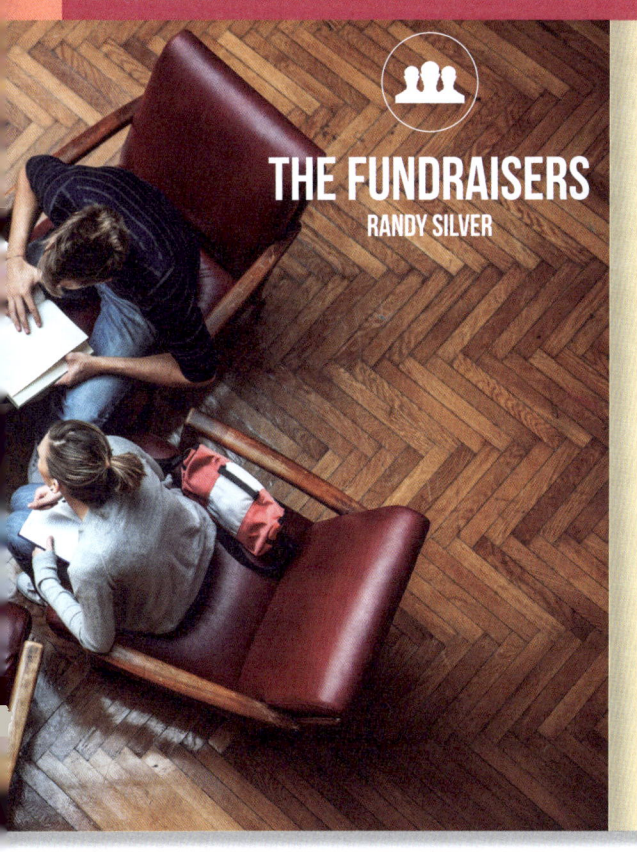

THE FUNDRAISERS
RANDY SILVER

* * * * *

Robbie said, "If we spend too much money on advertising, we'll have less to spend on helping people."

Maya said, "But if we spend too little on advertising, not enough people will come to our event! And that means we won't make much money anyway."

We had set up American Food Aid (or AFA, for short) so we could make a difference. But we couldn't stop arguing.

"Look," said Jess, "instead of worrying about how much we spend on advertising, let's get imaginative with whatever amount we manage to raise. Think about it. If we invested the money from our fundraising event, we would make even more money and help even more people."

"The AFA is not a business, Jess! If we were a business, we wouldn't be a charity," said Robbie.

"But if we don't think like a business, we won't make any money, Robbie!"

Suddenly, Maya laughed and said, "I just had a great idea!"

29

1 Read the excerpt from the novel *The Fundraisers*. Who would like to invest the money?

2 Complete the sentences. Is the verb after *if* always in the same tense?

a If we ___spend___ too much money on advertising, we ___'ll have___ less to spend on helping people.

b But if we _____ too little on advertising, not enough people _____ to our event!

c If we _____ a business, we _____ a charity.

d If we _____ the money from our fundraising event, we _____ even more money and help even more people.

e But if we _____ like a business, we _____ any money, Robbie!

73

Grammar: First and Second Conditionals

We use the first conditional to describe things that are real possibilities in the future. Sentences have *if* + verb in the present simple in one part and *will/won't* + base verb in the other part.

If we **win** the game, we**'ll be** in first place.
If it **doesn't stop** raining, we **won't be able** to go to the beach.
We**'ll have** the party in the garden **if** the weather **is** good.

We use the second conditional to describe situations in the present or future that are hypothetical, unlikely, or impossible. Sentences have *if* + verb in the past simple in one part and *would/wouldn't* + base verb in the other part.

If I **could** be an animal, I**'d be** a bird.
You **wouldn't feel** so tired if you **didn't stay** up so late.

3 Put the verbs in the box in the correct form to make first conditional sentences.

> click   give   work   ~~celebrate~~   go   catch

a We _____'ll celebrate_____ with our families if we win the tournament!
b If you _____ on that link, it'll take you to the right page.
c We _____ snowboarding if it snows this weekend.
d If you _____ hard, you'll all do well on your exams.
e I _____ you the book tomorrow if I finish reading it tonight.
f We _____ the bus if we run!

4 Use the verbs in the box to complete the text with sentences in the second conditional.

> give   ~~have~~   be   not know   be   have

If I 1 ___had___ a lot of money, I probably 2 _____ what to do with it. Would I spend it or save it? I don't think I'd do either. The truth is, I don't want to be rich. I want to live in a world where everyone has what they need, not one where a few people have everything. OK. That's my answer: If I 3 _____ rich, I 4 _____ my money away to people who are not as lucky as I am. I think that if everyone 5 _____ what they needed for a good life, the world 6 _____ a better place. Anyway, what about you? What would you do?

5 Make second conditional sentences.

a I / improve my Spanish / I / practice more
   I would improve my Spanish if I practiced more.

b I / not go to the party / I / finish my economics project
   _____.

c we / get the 5:30 train / we / not miss the start of the movie
   _____.

d I / go to San Francisco / I / walk across the Golden Gate Bridge
   _____.

e I / learn Mandarin / we / live in Beijing
   _____.

6 Complete the sentences with correct form of the word in parentheses. Sentences are in either the first or second conditional.

a I'd travel the world if I ____had____ a million dollars. (have)

b I'll go to the movie if I _____ my homework on time. (finish)

c I'll have enough to buy a guitar by the end of the year if I _____ the money I earn from my job at the sporting goods store! (save)

d I'll tell Ali about the party if I _____ him. (see)

e I'd visit the Mayan and Aztec ruins if I ever _____ to Mexico. (go)

f I'd learn Russian if we _____ in Russia. (live)

7 Answer the questions with your own ideas. In your answers, write complete first or second conditional sentences.

a If you had a lot of money, what would you do with it?
   _____.

b If you could live in any country, where would you live?
   _____.

c If the weather is good this weekend, what will you do?
   _____.

d If you do well on your next exams, how will you celebrate?
   _____.

Grammar: Third Conditional

Luca Jones and Maria Doyle lost a lot of money when their bookstore was forced to close. Our reporter, Janice Wilson, spoke to the couple.

For many years, the New Leaf Bookstore was a success. With its loyal customers and talks by famous authors, New Leaf was the heart of the small town of Ashbury. But over time, as people bought more e-books and bought more books online, fewer people went to New Leaf for their books, and eventually the store closed down.

Luca says they didn't think things through: "If we had known what was going to happen, we wouldn't have set up the business. If we had paid more attention to what was going on online, we wouldn't have gotten ourselves into this position."

Maria agrees, saying, "If smartphone technology hadn't come along, things would have been different. But it's just so easy to buy a book online now. If we had thought more about it, we would have opened the bookstore as a website." Smiling, Maria continues, "In fact, that's just what we're going to do. In the fall, we're opening up again—online. Luca's not quite so sure, but I think we can make it a success."

1 Read the article. What do Luca and Maria plan to do in the fall?

2 Complete the sentences. What form of the verb is used after *if*?

a If we _____had known_____ what was going to happen, we _____wouldn't have set up_____ the business.

b If we _____ more attention to what was going on online, we _____ ourselves into this position.

c If smartphone technology _____, things _____ different.

d If we _____ more about it, we _____ the bookstore as a website.

Grammar: Third Conditional

We use the third conditional to imagine a different past. We think of how things might have been different if something that happened in the past hadn't happened or if something that didn't happen had happened.

Third conditional sentences have *if* + verb in the past perfect in one part and *would/ wouldn't* + *have* + past participle of the verb in the other part.

If I had worked hard, **I would have passed** the exam. (I didn't work hard, and I didn't pass the exam.)

If I hadn't gone to Leo's birthday party, **I wouldn't have met** Pablo. (I did go to Leo's party, and I did meet Pablo.)

3 Put the verbs in parentheses in the correct form to make third conditional sentences.

a If I hadn't broken my leg, I 'd have played in the basketball tournament. (play)

b If we _____ late for swim practice, our coach wouldn't have been happy. (be)

c We _____ to Los Angeles if Mom had taken the job. (move)

d We'd have caught the bus if we _____ the house earlier. (leave)

e If I _____ all my money, I would have been able to buy those sneakers. (not spend)

f If you _____ , I would have helped you. (ask)

4 Complete the conversation. Complete the third conditional sentences with the verbs in the box in the correct form.

> choose   make   ~~work~~   not fail   think   enjoy

Dad   If you 1 had worked more this year, you 2 _____ your exams.

Josh I don't know, Dad. I think I chose the wrong subjects. If I 3 _____ art, English, and history, I 4 _____ school more.

Dad   Don't you like what you're studying?

Josh Not really. I think I made the wrong choices. Math, science, and geography are not for me. If I 5 _____ more carefully about it last year, I 6 _____ a better decision.

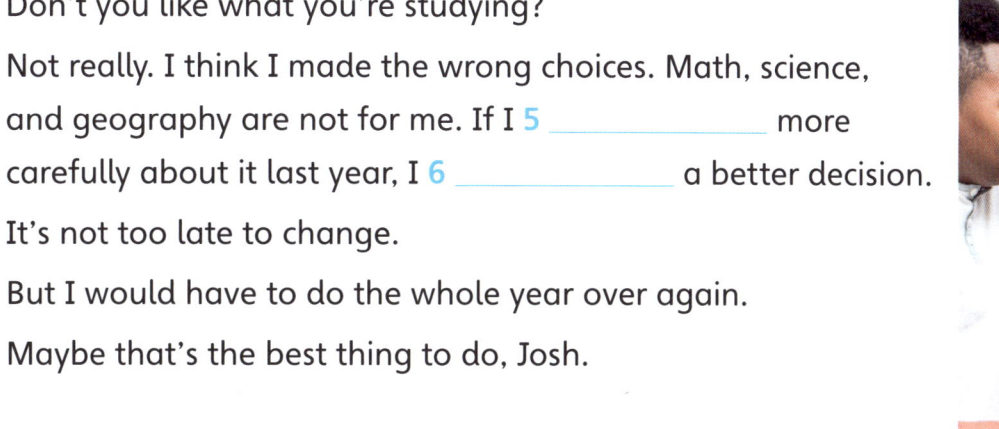

Dad   It's not too late to change.

Josh But I would have to do the whole year over again.

Dad   Maybe that's the best thing to do, Josh.

5) Make third conditional sentences.

a If / I / not go / to bed so late / I / not feel / so tired
   If I hadn't gone to bed so late, I wouldn't have felt so tired.

b If / I / have / enough money with me / I / buy / both jackets
   _____.

c If / it / rain / we / not go / to the beach
   _____.

d You / not feel / so hungry / if / you / eat / something for breakfast
   _____.

e I / go out / if / it / not be / so cold
   _____.

6) Read the situations. Use the third conditional to complete the sentences.

a We got up late. We didn't catch the train.
   If we hadn't gotten up late, we would have caught the train.

b It rained. We didn't have a picnic.
   _____.

c I lost my ticket. I didn't go the show.
   _____.

d I broke my brother's phone. He was angry with me.
   _____.

e I ate three pieces of chocolate cake. I felt sick.
   _____.

f The bus was late. I missed the start of the movie.
   _____.

7) How would your life have been different if you had gone to a different school instead of the school you go to? Write three sentences in the third conditional.

If I had gone to a different school, I wouldn't have met Mia and Emilio.
_____
_____

Improve Your Writing

Quantifiers and Subject–Verb Agreement

Quantifiers are words that indicate an amount of people or things. We use them with nouns. Examples include *all*, *each*, and *many*.

Each student **is** responsible for part of the presentation.

I have two laptops, but **one** of them **is** broken.

Most of the students in my class **have** a smartphone, but only **some** of them **have** a tablet.

Many of my friends **speak** two languages.

Some quantifiers agree just with singular verbs—for example, *one*, *each*.

Some quantifiers agree just with plural verbs—for example, *many*.

Some quantifiers agree with singular or plural verbs—for example, *all*, *most*, *some*. When choosing which verb to use with these quantifiers, look at the noun or pronoun after the quantifier. Choose a plural verb only for plural countable nouns or plural pronouns.

All of the **books are** on the shelf.

All of that **time was** wasted!

1 Circle the correct verb form.

a Some people **is** / (**are**) very good at learning languages.

b Most of your homework **was** / **were** OK, Jo, but take another look at the last page.

c Many people **spend** / **spends** their money instead of saving it.

d This is a confusing book. Some of it **seem** / **seems** to not make much sense at all.

e Each tablet **come** / **comes** with a pair of wireless headphones.

f One of my friends **want** / **wants** to be an actor.

g All of us is **going** / **are going** to the party on Saturday.

2 Complete the sentences with the correct form of the verb in parentheses.

a Many people ___think___ soccer players earn too much money. (think)

b One of my cousins _____ in Australia. (live)

c Each of the apartments in the building _____ five rooms. (have)

d Most people in my town _____ kind and friendly. (be)

e Some students at my school _____ we have too much homework. (say)

f Each after-school club _____ at 3 p.m. and lasts one hour. (start)

Writing: A Comparison Essay

1 READ Read the comparison essay. How many kids in the group usually save most of their allowance?

<u>The Allowance Survey</u>

We did a group survey about the allowance our parents give us. There were ten people in our group. We wanted to find out whether people are happy with the amount they receive, what they need to do at home to get their allowance, and what they do with the money.

We found that all of us get an allowance. Six of us are happy with the amount we receive, while four of us believe that our allowance is too low. All of us must help out at home in order to receive our allowance. The chores we do regularly include doing the dishes, taking out the garbage, and cleaning our bedrooms.

The main difference was what people do with their allowance. Half of us usually save most of it; the other half of us usually spend most of it. All of us believe it is important to save money. If, one month, we spend our whole allowance, all of us feel a little guilty.

In conclusion, each of us receives an allowance, but some of us are happy with the amount we receive and others aren't. In addition, only some of us manage to save a good amount of our allowance each month.

2 EXPLORE Match the parts of a comparison essay with the excerpts from "The Allowance Survey."

1   introduction to the survey   _____
2   key similarities in the survey   _____
3   key differences in the survey   _____
4   conclusion with short summary   _____

a   We found that all of us get an allowance.
b   Each of us receives an allowance, but some of us are happy with the amount we receive and others aren't.
c   We did a group survey about the allowance our parents give us.
d   Half of us usually save most of it; the other half of us usually spend most of it.

3 PLAN You are going to write a comparison essay about homework. First, talk to people in your class and complete the table below with your results of the survey.

How many people are there in the group?	
When do you do your homework? ● Number of people who do their homework as soon as they get home ● Number of people who leave their homework until the last minute ● Number of people who do their homework at other times (what times?)	
What's your opinion of the amount of homework? ● Number of people who think they have too much homework ● Number of people who think they have the right amount of homework	

4 WRITE Write your comparison essay. Use the information in Activity 3.

CHECK

Did you …
- write an introduction and a conclusion with a short summary? ☐
- include key similarities and differences? ☐
- use quantifiers, if possible? ☐

Practice Your Exam Skills

Read the text. Choose the best word (A, B, C, or D) for each space.

Money, Money, Money

Last year, I **1** _____ college and began working as a computer programmer. Since then, I have realized that there is one thing my education didn't give me—an understanding of money.

I know I should save money for my future, but as soon as I receive my **2** _____ each month, I think about things I can buy. My problem is simple: I **3** _____ money as soon as I earn it. It doesn't matter how expensive something is, I usually buy it, no matter what it costs. Why? Well, I work very hard to be **4** _____ at my job, and so I think I deserve to buy myself things: clothes, shoes, books.

However, I have a plan to change my attitude about money. Later this year, I am going to set up a **5** _____ business. This means I will have to stop spending money and start saving it. I already have my business **6** _____. My bank manager likes it. Now all I have to do is change my ways!

1	A retired	B left	C cleared	D went
2	A profit	B interest	C salary	D allowance
3	A invest	B spend	C pay	D get
4	A successful	B well	C lucky	D rich
5	A short	B tiny	C brief	D small
6	A plan	B drawing	C list	D map

9 How can we increase our brainpower?

Grammar: *if only*

THE BRAIN BLOG

POSTS | VIDEOS | LINKS | ABOUT ME

I'd asked Gran if she'd ever thought about how our brains work. She said, "Oh, if only you didn't think so much, Suzie, you'd have time to get things done." As you know, Brain Blog fans, I *love* to use my brain.

However, yesterday I learned that it isn't good to think about two things at the same time. I was in science class, holding a model of the human brain. I said, "If only we knew everything about how the brain works, we would be able to use it in new ways." I was thinking of the cerebellum when the model slipped from my hand. It cracked on the hard floor.

"Oh no!" I said. "I'm so sorry! I was thinking about nerve fibers and … "

"It's all right," said Miss Anderson.

"If only I had paid more attention," I thought, "I wouldn't have dropped it." Feeling terrible, I said, "If only I had held on to it firmly, it wouldn't have broken."

"I have another one in the cupboard," Miss Anderson said. "And it reminds me, Suzie. The brain is more efficient when we are using it to think about *one thing at a time*."

1 Read the blog post. What happens to the model of the brain?

2 Complete the sentences. Which are about the present and which are about the past? What tenses come after *if only*?

a If only you ___didn't___ think so much, Suzie, you ___'d have___ time to get things done.

b If only we _____ everything about how the brain works, we _____ use it in new ways.

c If only I _____ more attention, I _____ it.

d If only I _____ on to it firmly, it _____ .

Grammar: *if only*

We use *if only* to express a strong wish. It describes situations that we would like to be different.

If only for Situations in the Present:
if only + past simple verb, *would/could* + base verb

If only I could play the guitar, **I would join** Daniel's band.
If only I had more time, **I could learn** Mandarin.

If only for Situations in the Past:
if only + past perfect verb, *would* + *have* + past participle of verb

If only I had studied more, **I would have done** better on the test.

If only for Present Situations with Past Causes:
if only + past perfect verb, *would/could* + base verb

If only I hadn't lost my bag, **I would have** all my things now.
If only it had snowed last night, **we could ski** now.

3) Circle the correct verb.

a If only I (**had bought**) / **bought** that tennis racket last week, I could have brought it on our vacation.

b If only I **hadn't lost** / **didn't lose** my phone last weekend, I would still have all my photos.

c If only I **had had** / **had** more time now, I would learn to play the piano.

d If only it **hadn't rained** / **didn't rain** yesterday, we would have gone to the park.

e If only my friends **hadn't used** / **didn't use** social media all the time, we'd spend more time talking to each other face to face.

4) Complete the sentences with the correct form of the verbs in parentheses.

a If only I _____sang_____ well, I _____would get_____ a part in the school musical. (sing / get)

b If only I _____ more time last week, I _____ a cake for Mom's birthday. (have / make)

c If only we _____ so badly in the first thirty minutes of the final, we _____ the game. (not play / win)

d If only I _____ my brother's guitar last night, he _____ so mad at me now. (not break / not be)

e If only I _____ more time each day, I _____ my English more. (have / can practice)

5 Read the present situations with past causes. Complete the *if only* sentences.

a I didn't listen to the teacher. I don't know how to do the homework.
   If only I had listened to the teacher, I would know how to do the homework.

b I left my wallet at home. I can't buy the new tablet.
   _____, I could buy the new tablet.

c I didn't charge my phone. I can't use it to take photos.
   If only I had charged my phone, _____.

d I lost my key. I can't get into the house.
   _____, I could get into the house.

e It rained all night. The park is flooded.
   If only it hadn't rained all night, _____.

6 Read the past situations. Write sentences with *if only*.

a I didn't go on the website at the right time. I didn't get tickets to the concert.
   If only I had gone on the website at the right time, I would have gotten tickets to the concert.

b I didn't go to bed early. I felt so tired the next day.

c I arrived late at the train station. I missed my train.

d It rained last weekend. We couldn't go to the beach.

e I felt sick. I couldn't go to Kelsey's birthday party.

7 Think about your experience as a student of English now and in the past. What would you like to be different? Use *if only* and the past simple or past perfect.

If only I lived in the U.K. or the U.S.A., I'd be able to speak English more often.

85

Grammar: Modal Verbs of Deduction

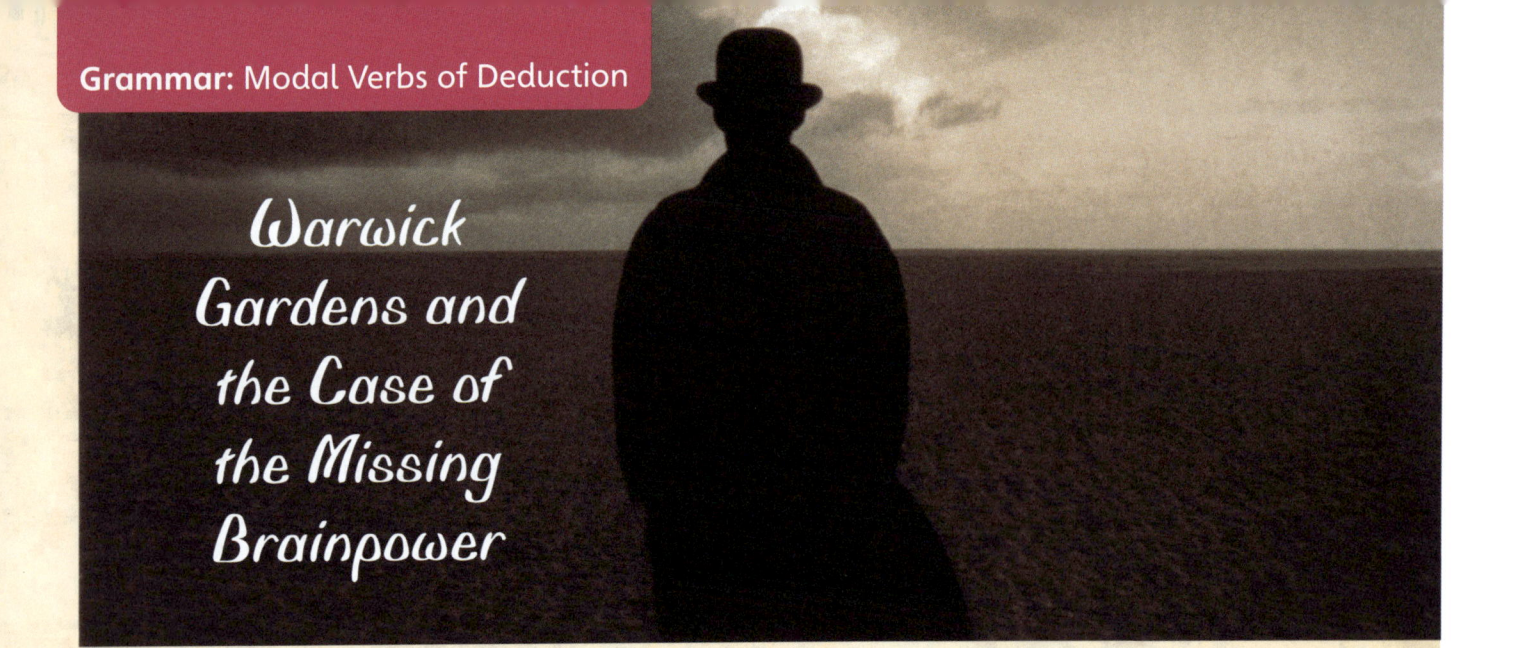

Warwick Gardens and the Case of the Missing Brainpower

CHAPTER ONE: The Idea

IT MUST HAVE BEEN MIDNIGHT BY THE TIME I GOT BACK TO BUTCHER STREET. THE MOON WAS HIGH, AND THE STREETS WERE QUIET. THERE WERE SO FEW PEOPLE AROUND THAT IT WAS AS IF I WAS THE ONLY PERSON ON THE PLANET. OF COURSE, I WASN'T: THE EARTH IS FULL. WHAT'S MORE, IT'S FULL OF CRIMINALS. ONE OF THEM, PROFESSOR JAMES, CONTINUES TO MAKE MY LIFE DIFFICULT. HOW HAD HE STOLEN THOSE PRICELESS JEWELS FROM THE MUSEUM OF ARCHEOLOGY? I HAD NO IDEA. HERE I WAS, THE WORLD'S GREATEST DETECTIVE, AND I COULDN'T MAKE SENSE OF IT.

"I NEED TO INCREASE MY BRAINPOWER," I SAID TO MY ASSISTANT, THOMPSON. "MY BRAIN ISN'T WORKING PROPERLY. HELP ME, THOMPSON. HOW DID JAMES DO IT? HE CAN'T HAVE BROKEN IN THROUGH THE FRONT GATE—THERE ARE GUARDS."

"HE MIGHT HAVE GONE IN THROUGH THE ROOF, WARWICK."

"HE CAN'T HAVE DONE THAT—THERE ARE SECURITY CAMERAS. THE MUSEUM IS VERY SAFETY CONSCIOUS."

"THEN IT'S SIMPLE, WARWICK," SAID THOMPSON. "HE MUST HAVE HAD HELP FROM SOMEONE AT THE MUSEUM."

"BRILLIANT! WHY DIDN'T I THINK OF THAT?"

"YOU'RE OVERWORKED, WARWICK. IT'S TIME YOU TOOK A BREAK."

"I WILL, AS SOON AS WE'VE CRACKED THIS CASE. NOW, NEXT QUESTION: WHO HELPED HIM?"

1 Read the detective story. Who works out how James must have stolen the jewels?

2 Complete the sentences. In which sentences is the speaker sure of what he is saying and in which is he unsure?

a He _____ broken in through the front gate—there are guards.

b He _____ gone in through the roof.

c He _____ done that—there are security cameras.

d He _____ had help from someone at the museum.

Grammar: Modal Verbs of Deduction

We use modal verbs of deduction plus a past participle to make guesses about the past.
must have: we use this when we are almost sure about something.
    The cat was out in the snow all night. She must have been freezing!
might have: we use this when we think something was possible but we are not at all sure.
    I can't find my phone. I might have left it at Jessica's house.
can't have: we use this when we are almost sure that something wasn't possible.
    It can't have been easy for Alessandro to change schools in the middle of the year.

3 Complete the sentences with *must have*, *might have*, or *can't have*.

   a I'm almost sure that I left my book at school.
      I _____must have_____ left my book at school.

   b It's a possibility that Jack went to the movies.
      Jack _____ gone to the movies.

   c It's a possibility that Mel fixed your computer.
      Mel _____ fixed your computer.

   d I'm almost sure you didn't see Sarah.
      You _____ seen Sarah.

   e I'm sure you were happy with your new bike.
      You _____ been happy with your new bike.

   f Where's the rest of the chocolate cake? I'm almost sure that Molly and Cleo didn't eat it all!
      They _____ eaten all the cake!

4 Complete the sentences with *must have*, *might have*, or *can't have* and the verbs in parentheses.

   a I'm almost sure that Oliver and Kate didn't do well on the test.
      They _____must have done_____ badly on the test. (do)

   b I'm almost sure it wasn't possible that I left my bag at school.
      I _____ my bag at school. (leave)

   c It's possible that my uncle and aunt got stuck in traffic.
      They _____ in the traffic. (get stuck)

   d I'm sure everyone on the team was thrilled when they won.
      Everyone on the team _____ thrilled when they won. (be)

   e It's possible that I forgot to put my homework in my bag.
      I _____ to put my homework in my bag. (forget)

5 Complete the sentences with *must have*, *might have*, or *can't have* and the words in the box.

> ~~be~~   get lost   leave   go   be

a You ____must have been____ so happy when you got your exam results. You did so well!

b I can't find my ticket anywhere. I haven't seen it since I left the house. I remember it was on my desk in my room. I _____ it there.

c Jim did really well. It _____ easy to speak in front of the whole school, but he was great!

d Tom _____ to the mall. He said he'd like some new sneakers.

e I wonder where they are. I'll give them a call. They _____ —they've been here so many times and know the area well.

6 Read the situations. Make deductions using *must have*, *might have*, or *can't have* and the verbs in parentheses.

a I don't know where my jacket is. Maybe it is at Sue's house. (leave)
I _might have left my jacket at Sue's house_.

b I went to Eliot's house and knocked on his door. There was no answer. (go out)
Eliot _____.

c The soccer game has finished. The kids look really happy. (win)
The team _____.

d I don't know who called. It's possible that it was Helen. (be)
It _____.

e I know I didn't leave my wallet on the bus—I had it when I got home. (leave)
I _____.

7 Read the situation. Make deductions using *must have*, *can't have*, and *might have*.

KARL DOESN'T KNOW WHERE HIS PHONE IS. HE HAD IT AT SCHOOL. HE ALSO HAD IT AFTER SCHOOL, WHEN HE AND GEORGIA WENT TO THE PARK. KARL ISN'T SURE IF HE USED HIS PHONE IN THE PARK, BUT HE REMEMBERS THAT GEORGIA USED IT BECAUSE HERS WASN'T CHARGED. IT WAS ONLY WHEN HE GOT BACK FROM THE PARK THAT HE REALIZED THAT HE DIDN'T KNOW WHERE HIS PHONE WAS.

_____

_____

Improve Your Writing

Reporting Verbs

Different reporting verbs are followed by different structures.
Verbs followed by *that* (announce, explain, shout)
   She explained that she had struggled with her science homework.
Verbs followed by object + infinitive *(tell, invite)*
   Dad told me to do my homework.
Verb followed by either *that* or infinitive *(say, agree, promise)*
   She said to be quiet. She said that she wanted to enjoy the film.
Remember that tenses, pronouns, and possessive adjectives change in reported speech.

1 Complete the sentences with *promised*, *announced*, *invited*, *told*, or *explained*.

a "I'll go to bed early."
   Sam _____promised_____ to go to bed early.

b "Robbie, be quiet!"
   Kate _____ her brother to be quiet.

c "I want to be a professional tennis player!"
   Amelia _____ that she wanted to be a professional tennis player.

d "No, Karlie. My dad isn't from Germany. He comes from Türkiye."
   George _____ that his dad came from Türkiye.

e "Would you like to come to my birthday party?"
   Lucas _____ me to his birthday party.

2 Report the statements. Use the words in parentheses.

a "I'm going to the movies."   (Wendy / say)
   Wendy said that she was going to the movies.

b "Clean up your room!"   (Mom / tell / me)
   _____

c "I'll clean the kitchen."   (Dad / promise)
   _____

d "I'm going to be a singer!"   (my brother / announce)
   _____

e "Work hard."   (the teacher / say)
   _____

Writing: A Memoir

1 READ Read Elena's description. What special memory is she describing?

I'll always remember the day I announced that I was going to be an actor. It was a Saturday, and we were in the kitchen at home. Mom and Dad had always wanted me to be a scientist, like them. But investigating the mysteries of the human brain was their work. I wanted to act!

I explained that I felt happy when I was pretending to be someone else, but they were worried about my plan. They said that I might spend a long time without work. However, when I told them that my drama teacher believed I was good enough to be a professional actor, they began to take me seriously.

We moved from the kitchen into the living room. Mom was drinking a coffee. Dad was holding a glass of water tightly in his hand. Dad asked if it was what I wanted to do more than anything else in the world. I said it was, and I promised to work really hard. Mom and Dad looked at each other, smiled, and agreed to support me. Nine years later, on the opening night of my first movie, they were there, prouder and happier than anyone else in that theater. My parents taught me how important it is to support your children in what they want to do.

2 EXPLORE Complete the text with the words in the box.

memory   past   experience   writer   events   ~~memoir~~   first person   diary

A 1 __memoir__ is a description of a particular 2 _____ or set of memories. It describes a person's own 3 _____ in the 4 _____. Written in the 5 _____, a memoir is often very personal and revealing, and is different from a 6 _____, in that it is usually written long after the 7 _____ being described. This gives the 8 _____ the chance to write about what their experience might have taught them.

3 PLAN
You are going to write a memoir. Think about an important or memorable experience in your life. Then, make notes on it below.

What Is the Experience?

Who Was Involved?

What Happened?

When and Where Did It Happen?

What Did the Experience Teach You?

4 WRITE
Write your memoir. Use the information.

CHECK

Did you …
- write about your own experience, saying what happened, when and where it happened, and what it taught you?
- write in the first person?
- include different reporting verbs (for example, *announced*, *explained*, *agreed*) with the correct structures?

Read the text. Choose the correct answer.

David Wilmot—The Man Who Never Forgets

When I tell people I have a photographic memory, they usually say that they would like to have one too. But I wouldn't mind if I didn't have this type of memory. Yes, it can be very useful to never forget anything, but there are also disadvantages.

I first realized that my memory was not the same as other people's when I was in elementary school. I would get 100% on tests of knowledge. The teachers thought that I studied hard, but they were wrong. I didn't have to study hard before an exam; I just had to remember what I had been told. As soon as I learned something, I knew it and never forgot it.

These days, I find having a photographic memory can make me sad. This is because I remember things that other people don't, which means that I can't share these memories. But I suppose the worst part is that I have far too much information in my head, a lot of it not very important!

1 In elementary school, David
   A studied hard for tests.
   B found out that his memory was different.
   C didn't know he had a photographic memory.
   D didn't do well on tests of knowledge.

2 What does David say about elementary school?
   A He didn't enjoy his time there.
   B He couldn't remember anything in class.
   C He struggled on tests.
   D It didn't take him long to learn something.

3 How does David feel about his photographic memory now?
   A He enjoys sharing his memories with others.
   B He is pleased to remember everything.
   C He says that not everything he remembers matters.
   D He wishes he could remember even more than he can.

4 What would be a good introduction to the article?
   A Over time, David Wilmot realized that there were good and bad things about a photographic memory.
   B David Wilmot explains why having a photographic memory is so enjoyable.
   C In this article, David Wilmot tells us how his teachers discovered his amazing memory.
   D David Wilmot explains how his memories have brought him closer to his friends.

Review: Units 1-3

Read the text. Choose the right words and write them in the blanks.

All green-hued envy and red-orange fear

Is the man **0** ___who___ screams, but no one can hear.

Loud as the sunset and dull **1** _____ the moon

A sound **2** _____ ripples all that is near.

3 _____ a shriek that the lines seem to blend into one

An open-mouthed thunder, **4** _____ will never be done,

So sad **5** _____ the others want **6** _____ into blue

And see **7** _____ turn toward the elegant hue

Of the one **8** _____ mouthed Os of **9** _____ agonized pain

Are noiselessly echoed and **10** _____ in vain.

0	whose	who	which
1	as	such	so as
2	who	which	that
3	So	Such	Such that
4	that	who	which
5	that	who	which
6	to blend	to blended	blend
7	themselves	himself	herself
8	who	who's	whose
9	such	so	very so
10	will being echoed	will echoed	will be echoed

Review: Units 4–6

Read the text. Choose the right answers and write them in the blanks.

Dad told me **0** ____to be____ careful.
I **1** _____ it his way. But I wanted to see the kittens.
When I entered the old house, the back door already
2 _____ shut. I tried the other **3** _____.
It slammed shut, too! I was stuck!
I had to find **4** _____ way out **5** _____
there wasn't any!
SLAM! Who's that? "Heeeellllpp!"
I heard Jack: "Bri, Dad asked me **6** _____ on you."
On the one hand, I **7** _____ to Dad
8 _____ he's usually right. **9** _____,
I wanted to see the kittens. Still, **10** _____ the kittens
soon—but with Dad this time!

0	was	to be	be
1	could have did	could have done	should done
2	has closed	had closed	closes
3	one	any	some
4	one	some	no
5	!	;	.
6	to check	checking	have checked
7	could have listen	would have listened	should have listened
8	when	because	so
9	On the one hand	On the hand	On the other hand
10	I be seeing	I'll be seeing	I won't be seeing

Review: Units 7–9

Read the text. Choose the right words and write them in the blanks.

We **0** _had been gardening_, and after we cleaned ourselves up, she asked me to go upstairs with her. She announced **1** _____ she had a surprise for me. She opened up her old wooden jewelry box. It was full of sparkling pieces. Each of them **2** _____ special. All of them **3** _____ beautiful. Grandma drew out an antique necklace and handed it to me. She asked if I would take care of it, and I promised that I would. I knew that it **4** _____ to her by her grandmother.

If only I hadn't been so eager to wear it, I **5** _____ grandma's necklace to Alice's party. If I **6** _____ the clasp fixed **7** _____ I went, I wouldn't have lost it. It **8** _____ fallen off at home or at Alice's house because I would have found it. I **9** _____ it on the way.

I lost that necklace, but, if I have the chance, I **10** _____ something special to my grandchild, too. The memory I have of that afternoon with my grandmother is more valuable to me than that necklace ever was.

0	have been gardening	had gardened	had been gardening
1	when	that	which
2	are	was	were
3	are	was	were
4	have been given	had given	had been given
5	would have worn	wouldn't have worn	wouldn't wear
6	hadn't had	had had	have had
7	after	since	before
8	could have	can have	can't have
9	must have lost	must lose	mustn't lose
10	won't give	will give	will have given

Thanks and Acknowledgments

The authors and publishers acknowledge the following sources of copyright material and are grateful for the permissions granted. While every effort has been made, it has not always been possible to identify the sources of all the material used or to trace all copyright holders. If any omissions are brought to our notice, we will be happy to include the appropriate acknowledgments on reprinting and in the next update to the digital edition, as applicable.

Photography

All the photographs are sourced from Getty Images.

Cover photography by Gonzalo Azumendi/Stone/Getty Images; JAH/iStock/Getty Images; Rapeepong Puttakumwong/Moment/Getty Images.

Illustration

Collaborate Agency.

Cover illustrations by Sara Gianassi (Astound).

Typesetting

Blooberry Design and QBS Learning.